Hinduism Redefined

About the Author

A.P. Sharma, born at Dholpur, Rajasthan on 25th Dec., 1932, graduated from Agra College Agra in 1954, joined Maharaja's College at Jaipur and obtained post-graduates degree in English literature. He also obtained post-graduate degrees in Education and philosophy in 1966 and 1969 respectively, as also Ph.D. degrees in Educaton and Philosophy from the Rajasthan University. After serving the Department of Education in Rajasthan University for almost 15 years, he proceeded to Nigeria to join Sokoto University as a Senior Lecturer and became Associate Reader at the University before he left for India around 1985. The same year he was appointed as a Principal of RMV College of Education at Udaipur. After a couple of years, he shifted to IASE Vidyabhawan, Udaipur and joined there as a Professor of Educational Philosophy. Later on, he also visited Willamette University at Salem, Oregon, USA. So far he has written 22 books and 65 articles. He has guided seven Ph.D. scholars successfully.

HINDUISM REDEFINED

A.P. SHARMA

CONCEPT PUBLISHING COMPANY, NEW DELHI-110059

ISBN: 81-8069-082-2 (HB)

First Published 2004

Published and Printed by
Ashok Kumar Mittal
Concept Publishing Company,
A/15-16, Commercial Block, Mohan Garden,
New Delhi-110059 (INDIA)

Phones : 25351460, 25351794
Fax : 091-11-25357103
Email : publishing@conceptpub.com

Dedicated to

SWAMI VIVEKANANDA

Preface

It is really difficult to trace the time when the dawning of Hinduism started. The Western and the Indian scholars differ in this respect. The more we read about it, the more complicated the issue becomes as the exact dates of the beginning and growth of the religion are not known. Still it is considered by a number of scholars that the religion started sometime during two to three thousand years before Christ. In view of that, it has been my sincere efforts to trace the history of Hinduism from as close an angle as possible. My basic concentration has been on the issues, precepts and the beliefs that finally culminated into a religion known as Hinduism.

The first chapter is, therefore, totally devoted to the historical background of the religion starting from the Indus Valley Civilization through Vedic and Brahmanic periods to the rise of Hinduism, both classical and modern. All this has been done through extensive research and after collecting the material very carefully. In fact, most people know only vaguely about the beginning of the religion. There are many books, which deal with different kinds of gods, goddesses and religious practices in Hinduism. But there is hardly any authentic book, which unfolds how the human beliefs developed from the ancient to the modern times and formed into one religion. Thus, the first chapter deals with all that and marks distinctly that Hinduism, though mostly understood as a way of life, has a history of its own and can be conceived as one of the greatest religions of the world.

The second chapter deals with how Hindu beliefs have been emanated. Starting with inadequate interpretations of Hinduism by some Western and even eastern scholars, I have developed the chapter enumerating the process of inception of the beliefs. It is the most interesting part of the book, as a great number of people, who claim to belong to the religion, still don't know how actually the Hindu beliefs started. The chapter deals with when and how the beliefs got matured. It also deals with how Hinduism as a liberal religion project varied ways of liberation. In this respect, it is one of the unparalleled religion of the world.

The third chapter unfolds the best in the religion. Although its certain inadequacies have also been projected, it contains extensively the best in the religion. Everything that is peerless in religion, that include liberalism, variety not stagnation, implicit kindness, Hinduism as a accommodating religion etc. have been discussed. What are good reasons for visiting the four dhams, stress on moral conduct, duty for duty's sake, multiple ways of liberation, and rich philosophical background and literature have also been highlighted in it quite extensively and intimately.

The fourth chapter is partially an outcome of research and includes opinions of couple of hundreds of people in India and abroad. It focuses on what a Hindu is expected to do today. It contains how new customs and traditions have cropped up into the system, why people have apathy to visiting temples, corruption at holy places, lack of availability of the experts in religion, and what is really expected of a Hindu in a situation of current turmoil, etc. What is the way to solve these problems and save the religion from getting polluted from the rapid changes that are taking place on account of the new practices adopted by the people? These are some of the issues that have been highlighted in it. Besides, it also contains what a Hindu is required to do? And what he must do to remain aliened with the religion to help perpetuating it smoothly?' The definition of Hinduism is redefined precisely to enable each Hindu-minded person to keep in view what Hinduism is in reality.

I strongly feel that such material is the need of the day. If the reader goes through it patiently, the book will have a greater reception. I don't promise that I have given every thing that belongs to Hinduism, for opinions vary person to person, but I am confident that I have given what I thought to be the most intense and important. I hope the reader will like my approach in reprojecting Hinduism from a different but solemn angle. At this point I sincerely express my thanks to a number of my friends for reading the manuscript dispassionately and reflecting on the issues that were most crucial to be added to the text. I would not have been able to present it in its present shape if an objective assessment of these friends had not been a positive factor to make me conclude it in this manner.

CAMAS (Washington), USA **A. P. Sharma**
March 29th, 2003

Acknowledgements

The author gratefully acknowledges the work of the authors like Michel Darton and Peter Bishop, Keith Crim, Gavin Flood, Norman Anderson and Brandon whose research findings on Hinduism provided him the basic knowledge about the advent of the religion. He also desires to thank sincerely all those whom he interviewed round the world for they candidly supplied unbridled information about the religion. He is equally thankful to the members of his family, especially those who inspired him to complete the work and provided him different kinds of amenities that helped complete this humble work. The author is also thankful to Sri Ashok Kumar Mittal, the publisher, who thankfully accepted this work for he believes that it would benefit all those who strongly desire to know about their own religion from a different angle.

Contents

Chapter One

The Advent of Hinduism

The Dawning

Hinduism is one of the major religions of India and, at the same time, one of the oldest faiths of the world. Hinduism is the religion of the majority of people in India and Nepal. Today, Hindus are also found in many other countries of Asia, Africa and the West. Total number of Hindus in the entire world is estimated at over 1000 millions.

Hindus originally described their own religious beliefs and practices as *sanatan dharma,* which meant the 'eternal law', for Hinduism is believed to be eternal and unchanging. It is reckoned that Hinduism has gradually evolved over a period of three millennia. It includes many different beliefs, which consist of most elementary to the most highly developed philosophical and theological ideologies. Thus, Hinduism is an umbrella kind of term indicating to an amalgamation of varied religious beliefs sharing the essential qualifications.

It is really difficult to trace its origin because it is lost in the distant past. It possesses no single founder and no central doctrine. Neither it has a unified organization or transmission of teaching. Its main transporters were the bonds of family, caste and village life that bound the people in one thread in spite of their different beliefs and practices.

Until the culmination of the nineteenth century, Hinduism was not a missionary religion but primarily it had an ethnic character. Whatever its diversities are, it is much more than a religion. It influences the entire way of life and thereby has shaped a great civilization. In spite of its complex internal diversities, Hinduism can be considered as a complete whole, embracing all aspects of human life. It covers social, religious, economic, artistic, literary aspects and reflects a cultural ancestry of immense richness.

Hinduism has a great tradition of learning. It possesses a great store of philosophical and religious literature, which has been created and sincerely handed over and transmitted through the centuries by the learned class known as Brahmans. The practices of the Brahmans are sometimes known as Sanskritic because most of it is contained in texts written in Sanskrit language. In spite of that, most of Hinduism, as practised by the majority of Hindus, is based on local and regional traditions, which are often diverse in practice but not in principle.

It would be really incorrect to say that one can identify a separate village or a district, which would be completely influenced by the philosophy of Hinduism. Hindu diversity is so great that it includes many different elements from philosophical to theological to copious folk beliefs and practices as well as distinct influences from tribal groups that were imbibed into the society. The whole range of Hinduism from simple folk beliefs to practical ideology can be found in Indian villages and cities. It is because of that that there are strong regional differences in Hindu religious practices. Therefore, one can always find exceptions and disagreements to what is stated about Hinduism.

The systematic and important study of the Hindu religious traditions began only at the dawn of the nineteenth century. During this period some Western thinkers and outstanding Hindu scholars and reformers put tremendous efforts to discover what was not known to the majority of people about Hinduism. Through their efforts the handed down separate religious as well as philosophical beliefs were presented in a more associated manner. Consequently, the view of life in Hinduism has become clearer today. However, though much has been achieved today by way of better understanding of the various and varied aspects of Hinduism, many facets of the Hindu religion, tradition and the deep religious resources of this ancient faith still need further investigation.

Historical Perspective

Hinduism had its primary beginnings in two distinct sources that date from sometime in the third millennium B.C. to the middle or late second millennium B.C. The first is the Indus Valley Civilization that is linked with the cities known as Harappa and Mohanjo-Daro (now in Pakistan). Excavations of these well planned cities made during 1920s disclose that there existed highly developed system of life even before the appearance of the primary source of Hinduism, that is the Aryans and their oral scriptures, the Vedas. Since then, the Indian religion has gone through various periods of change that slowly created a consciousness of the single religion known as Hinduism. Broadly, the periods of change can be categorized as under two sets. One starting with the Indus Valley Civilization and ending with the advent of Orthodoxy in the religion. The other set starts with the rise of Hinduism and goes until the modern times when we witness Hinduism developing along with modern thinking. These sets, comprised of different periods, are listed here under:

The first set of development

1. Indus Valley Civilization
2. Vedic religion
3. Brahmanical religion
4. Divergent movements
5. Beginning of Orthodoxy

The second set of development

6. Rise of Hinduism
7. Classical Hinduism
8. Prevalence of Theism
9. Reactions against other religions
10. Modern Hinduism

The above broad divisions of the growth of Hinduism have been drawn after a lot of research and analysis but the entire period of this growth starts from such a distant past that there lies possibilities of many unaccounted gaps that would have taken place between each period. Besides, the interpretations that have been made after excavations and research are many a times inadequate as deciphering of the dug out material and reaching a complete conclusion on that basis cannot be considered totally accurate. Many of the results are simply generalizations. Still whatever decisions have been reached after such a gap of time with thoughtful considerations and great analysis, they are quite satisfactory to provide us absolutely a good idea of the religion and the culture that thrived during that time. I start from Mohanjo-Daro and Harappa and examine how people were culturally advanced and what kind of religion they practised.

(i) The Indus Valley Civilization

Indus valley civilization, usually referred to as the Harappa culture, was a highly developed urban civilization. The scholarly interpretations of the Indus valley or Harappa civilizations are at best uncertain, as the small number of known inscriptions still need to be deciphered. The exact nature of the function of many the compositions and structures in the cities is unknown. Small pieces of *terra cotta* and stone sculpture that have been found unfold the stories primarily connected with the animals, with emphasis upon the male. While representations of humans emphasize upon the female. Soapstone seals have also been discovered. They skillfully reproduce animals and in some cases they give emphasis on trees. There are also human figures projected in elementary form. But female figures are more prominently represented. Many female figures are specially dressed and are in dancing poses. These representations also indicate that the people of Indus valley seemed to possess a strong interest towards a very prominent female figure, like a Mother Goddess cult. The findings at the valley indicate that there was a clear emphasis upon water baths, drainage and personal cleanliness, having an inclination that Harappa religion concentrated upon natural powers. The essential role of water was to clean the people so that they might approach and be in proper relationship with the natural powers.

Still no knowledge of a system of thought, oral tradition or myth have been unfolded by the findings to support the idea that the people of Harappa civilization had a belief in some kind of a cult. It is simply the conjecture of the scholars that there was an awareness of powers different from or superior to humans. Many scholars hold that the Aryans came to India in the Northwest. It was probably the second millennium B.C. By then the Indus valley civilization had almost disappeared. Still the basic religious emphasis upon animals, trees and water continued to survive in some form, which later on constituted some aspects of Hinduism.

(ii) The Vedic Religion

The Aryans brought with them Sanskrit language, horse and chariot, including a sacrificial system known as Brahmanism or Vedism. It is inferred by the scholars that there are hardly any remains left belonging to the *Vedic* period that roughly started from 1500-600 B.C. But whatever is known about the *Vedic* religion must be inferred from the literary heritage of the Aryans, especially from their earliest collection, the *Rig Veda*. It is a collection of *hymns* in Sanskrit, composed over several centuries and reaching its final form around 900 B.C. The four *Vedas* and many later ritual and philosophical texts called *Brahmans* and *Aranyakas* developed into the philosophical dialogue of the *Upanishads.*

The Aryans were a part of the great migrations that spread to the shore of the Atlantic in the West and to Central and South Asia in the East. These wandering tribes, when settled down in the Northwestern region of India, subsequently provided societal, linguistic and religious traditions to the people in view of the climatic conditions and facilities unfolded to them by the nature. The Aryans were a martial people whose practices were patriarchal. As a result, their main divinities were male gods, mostly related to sky, the atmosphere and other natural forces. Later on, the rain god was also associated with them.

In fact, whatever we know about the Aryans' religion is known to us through the collection of *hymns* known as the *Vedas*. For a pretty long time after its origin, the *Vedic* literature was oral rather than written. The truth is that since the inception of the *Vedic* literature down to the modern times, the devout Hindus have been highly concerned with the accuracy of the text just to ascertain and absorb the truths the literature embodies. Originated from Sanskrit, the word *Veda* denotes knowledge. The *Vedic* literature during the course of time came to be understood as divinely revealed word or knowledge, that contains the truth of all existence and of all time. There are four major collections of the *Vedas* known as the ***Rig***, the ***Yajur***, the ***Sam*** and the ***Atharva*** *Vedas*. The *Rig Veda* contains the verses of praise for the supernatural. The *Yajur Veda* contains the sacrificial formulas to be used by the priests. The *Sam Veda* contains verses or chants for the priests to be used at the time of sacrifices. And the *Atharva Veda* is primarily a collection of verses concentrating upon spells and magical means to fulfil human desires in this world.

The religion revealed by the *Vedas* is mainly concerned about the sacrifices that have to be made to different gods residing in the form of nature or in the heavens. The gods are conceived as powers in the heaven, in the ambience and in the earth. They are also conceived as divine counterparts to the priests, rulers and people. The human society is dependent on the gods for maintaining the right order, which in other words is truth. This right order is maintained by human society observing strictly the sacrificial practices that are described in the *Vedas*. Consequently, the *Vedic* religion was highly sacrificial in nature and practice. At the same time, there is also a great emphasis on the material aspect of the world and human life, which made the physical also important. If the humans observed the ritualistic practices, it would make them materially happy in this life. As a result, observance of the rituals became the part of people's lives.

(iii) The Brahmanical Religion

This period of the history of the Aryans is dominated by the practice of sacrifices that were listed in the *Vedic* literature. The *Brahmans* or the priestly commentaries upon the *Vedic* verses served as guides for the priests. These commentaries contained detailed instructions for the proper performance of the sacrifices. Since it was a fundamental belief of the Aryans that sacrifices were absolutely necessary and required to be performed constantly to maintain the order in the universe as well as in the society, they made sacrifices regularly. The Brahman texts as well as the priests, who knew them well, came to hold almost divine status in the Brahmanic society.

Although it is absolutely not very easy to determine the specific periods in Indian history, it was perhaps the beginning of the first millennium B.C. when one of the main aspects of Brahmanic Hinduism developed. It was an emphasis upon a proper relationship between human society and divine powers. There laid the central role of the priests who acted as true guides in the conduct of the ritualistic practices necessary for the attainment and continuation of the relationship between the humans and the gods. The different gods, who controlled cosmic powers and maintained their supremacy on the powers of nature, must be pleased by the sacrifices apt to them. That would help maintain the cosmic order.

The role of society and individual was an essential matter to maintain the traditions so that the cosmic order could be well maintained. Gradually, performing the ritualistic practices by the individual as well as by the society was conceived as *dharma*, which roughly meant as one's obligations towards the gods for the maintenance of the proper order in the world. This conviction that all human activity has proper cosmological, ontological and divine patterns to follow became a fixed ideal in the development of the Indian religious practices. The divinities were appeased through a complex ritual of sacrifices thought essential in the adoption of the natural order of universe. It gave the priestly class (Brahmans) a great power and prestige.

During the period of the *Aranyakas* and the *Upanishads*, the culture nurtured by the Aryans penetrated further east into the plains in the vicinity of the river Ganges and reported to have reached up to Bengal. Some new beliefs appeared during this time. Perhaps, it must have been the impact of the indigenous inhabitants who lived at the plains of the Ganges during that time. One of the most important of these doctrines was the belief in transmigration or rebirth. This sort of belief was preceded with the idea that death also occurred in the heaven and the gods were also subjected to death. Finally, it was believed that all human beings die and take birth again. It was because of the frequent death and birth, there appeared the need of a final release from this world. Thus, it gave birth to the idea and belief in the attainment of *moksha.* We shall discuss how beliefs grew and developed in Hinduism at a later stage when we have done with the historical development of Hinduism.

Besides the emphasis on sacrifices, a lot of stress was given to 'correct' and 'proper' practices while invoking gods or making sacrifices during the early centuries of the first millennium B.C. With that, much consciousness and concern also grew about 'how to obtain the knowledge of the divine structure and what was man's relationship to it.' The sacrificial rituals demanded a highly trained group of priests who could follow and interpret the *Vedas* and the *Brahmans* properly. At this time certain individuals, who had the bent of mind and possessed right kind of intellectual wisdom, began to search for the hidden and unexplored knowledge in the *Vedas* and the sacrifice as well. Gradually, the meaning of the sacrifice came to be more important than its actual performance. It led to the development of a mental performance of the sacrifice that made the individual attain for himself the power of the sacrifice in an even greater degree than the priest who performed it. For most of the part, the priest who performed the rituals did not know its meaning and purpose well. Thus, as a result of man's desire to know more and to do good led him to excel and grow. Hinduism also developed like that.

There are legendary stories that convey how individuals

by performing *tapas* (a process of acquiring heat) acquired power to do the impossible. Examples of Ravana and many Rishies (mendicants) are quite popular in this respect. The *Rig Veda* in certain hymns refers to *tapas* as a basic element of power in creation. *Tapas* came to be in possession of the priests. A priest performed the sacrifice as a creative force to sustain the universe. The individual, who could perform the sacrifice as he had the right knowledge about it, was able to possess the unique power of the *tapas*.

The literature that developed to enhance such kind of knowledge came into existence as appendices to the *Brahmans*. It was known as *Aranyakas,* which was also known as 'Forest Books'. The individuals or the groups, who often retreated in the forests, used them. Besides the Vedas, the *Aranyakas* actually set the stage of the Hindu philosophy and theology. They contain a lot of philosophical speculations and queries about the ritualistic practices and difficult questions relating to human life. These early sources of the development of Indian religion during the period 1000-800 B.C. became instrumental in establishing certain fundamental elements within the emerging Hinduism. The Aryan-Vedic-Brahmanism, that emphasized greatly on sacrifice as the part of religion, also stressed on the requirement of ritual cleanliness while approaching the heavenly powers, which manifested in animals, rivers, etc. As man's faith grew on the validity of the knowledge contained in the *Vedas* and the *Aranyakas*, it led to the founding of certain main theories as fundamental truth of the cosmic and empirical existence. These concepts, that grew as a consequence to the acknowledgement of the *Vedic* knowledge, were mainly three:

1. Estimating sacrifice primarily to the great gods or powers of the universe;
2. Worship and fear to the natural powers that intercepted in man's daily life; and
3. A growing faith that intelligent reflections upon the *Vedic* truth can bestow man with the *tapas* (power). It would enable him to transcend human limitations.

Each of these elements continued as a central factor in the development of the Indian religion, which, later on, came to be known Hinduism. One must keep in mind that beliefs don't occur in man's mind without any reasons whether they may be flimsy or valid. Some beliefs originate on account of unknown fears and some spring up as a result of not been able to decipher the meaning of an awful thing vested in nature or human conduct. Thus, belief in sacrifice to appease gods came into being. How certain ancient individuals obtained power from *tapas*, performed by chanting certain prescribed text, is a matter of great research in the modern scientific age. It could be true as powerful words have definite impact and meaning too. Still, it can only be validated through some investigations by maintaining the prescribed mental wavelength and by chanting properly and accurately the verses (*mantras*) that helped obtain certain supernatural powers. What we see these days during certain occasions when the priest chants the holy verses is perhaps a kind of replica of the real activity. It is perhaps because of that that the desired results are not obtained. However, it is still a matter of research to prove or to disprove it.

It was in the early centuries of the first millennium B.C. that certain powerful concepts concerning human life and fate became important to the Indian religion. These concepts or basic beliefs came into being so powerfully that they became central to the Hindu religious speculations. They played major roles in the composition of Hinduism and later on Buddhism, as they were essential themes in Indian religion and philosophy. Both Jainism and much later Sikhism too were greatly influenced by these beliefs in certain ways. In fact, they served as theological and philosophical dogmas for Hinduism, but for the other religions e.g. Jainism and Sikhism, they worked as a source to reject one or more of the particular themes, giving them a status of a different religion from Hinduism. Consequently, these themes served as positive or negative factors and remained important with Indian religious thought that matured during the centuries.

Since these themes became important, they started

projecting human life as full of pain and struggle. The primary concepts (themes) which become popular with the people are those of rebirth, *samsara* and *karma*. Accordingly, they teach that individual souls exist from the beginning of time and go on existing from one form to the other continuously through rebirth and death. The existence of each new form depends on the merits and demerits of the actions (*karma*) that have taken place in previous life or existence. It was because of this kind of thinking about life that the religious thinkers started seeing life as frustrating since it was always involved with unending struggles, failures and defeats. Again, birth and death are inevitable consequences of human *karma*. When man acts, a chain of reactions crops up giving birth to other actions. Thus, each human being is involved in a chain of actions and reactions. Therefore, action is the cycle of *karma* and the process of rebirth and death is the inherent nature of all existence. That, in fact, is the nature of *samsara*.

Since these concepts came to be understood as the fundamental truth about human life and the cosmos, new developments within the Indian religious thought started growing as reactions to such ideologies. From the beginning of the eighth century B.C., the primary development within Indian religious thought was the attempt to find ways and means to get redeemed from the frustrating situations of life that included constant and continuous pain which was experienced on account of death and rebirth. Though the emphasis upon the sacrifice and keeping harmonious relationship with the gods did not lessen, there grew a belief that humans can come to terms with the cosmic existence. This kind of thought process served as basis for religious thought associated with later Hinduism. It also furnished many new ideas, both positive and negative, to the other religious movements such as Buddhism and Jainism that cropped up during the fifth century B.C.

The literature associated with this sort of development of thought was known as the *Upanisads*. It is believed to have developed before the fifth century B.C. The central theme of the *Upanisads* is that the *Vedas* are *Sruti*, that which is heard. They have been revealed directly to ancient *Rishis* (wise men).

Therefore, they contain absolute truth. Such beliefs are also common in the Western religions. There are passages in the *Brahmans* that convey that the *Vedas* have divine origin. It is also confirmed by certain passages contained in the *Upanisads*. The important thought contained in these holy books is that the Ultimate, the Divine has revealed truth to humans through the *Vedas*. The only goal of the *Upanisads* is to know this truth. Besides, there are other aspects of knowledge that must be understood by each individual if he/she wants to get rid of the pains that lie in continuous rebirth and death. It is that behind the multiplicity of the existence in the world there lies a unity that pervades it. This unity is even behind and above the various gods. It is known as Brahman, which is also understood as consciousness or a continuing power that upholds the total structure of the universe. But this Brahman must not be confused with any of the deities of the *Vedas*. The truth is that these gods are dependent on Brahman. They possess their power and position in the structure of the universe on account of Brahman only. Since it was impossible to see or understand Brahman from the ordinary human eye or mind, the *Upanisadic* theologians were conscious of the mysteriousness of Brahman. So they defined Brahman as pervading all the existence and greater than any individual and or the entire existence.

The concept of Brahman upheld by the *Upanisads* from the beginning was identified with *atman*, which meant 'self' or the 'inner self'. Thus, the term Brahman or *atman* is the source of all existent things, all essential energies, deities and all beings, and therefore, Brahman, Self or *atman* is the only Real of the real. It is at this point that Brahman is described in a way of series of negations, i.e. 'it is not this neither it is this', etc. We shall discuss it in details at a later stage. Gradually, as human speculations about religion extended, the search for a more pragmatic and satisfactory meaning of the term Brahman or *atman* began. Within the *Upanisads* a new dimension of the term Brahman stared getting meaning. It was that Brahman somehow manifest in the human person. This laid the ground of the later Vedanta (end of the Veda). It was the highest teaching of the Veda, which referred to as the understanding of the nature of person. It meant that if a person could reach the correct knowledge, which is the knowledge of his ultimate self, he would certainly come close to comprehending Brahman.

The *Upanisadic* theologians held that the inmost self of a person (*atman*) lies deep within. Next, they thought to strip away the physical and psychical elements from the *atman* as they stood at the surface to constitute the person. This ideology laid a firm philosophical and theological foundation for the ensuing intelligent formulations of popular Hinduism.

Obviously, next to it should have been the human concern to overcome the human situation that results from the *karma-samsaric* limitation. In other words, it was an urgent need to discover a way to end the chain of rebirth and death to get redeemed from the pain and suffering that results from the rebirth. Was there no way to get relieved from the chain of the rebirth and death and the wandering of the self through the endless time? Could there be a permanent release or *moksha* from the endless wandering, that seems to be an essential characteristic of the worldly being? The concept of permanent release first appears in the *Upanisads* but there is no absolute uniformity on the subject. The later commentaries and schools of philosophy with the passage of time developed various interpretations on the concept of *moksha*. So also the *Upanasadic* teachings developed various procedures about the release of the self from the *samsaric* (worldly) fetters, considering it as the final goal of human life. Most of these dogmas, that developed during the eighth century to the fifth century B.C., are still in vogue with the modern Hinduism and are held very precious by a Hindu whether he is deeply religious or not.

(iv) The Divergent Movements

The preceding centuries witnessed the growth of the priestly religion, which with the passage of time became more dogmatic in its practices. In its approach for cultivating good relationship with the gods and to maintain cosmic balance between the humans and the powers of the heaven, it strongly recommended sacrifice. Thus, strictly accomplishing the rituals became the way of life with the Indian religion by the middle of the sixth century. But gradually, it paved the way of revolt against those practices. There were a number of developments in religious thought and practice that greatly diverged from the Vedic-Brahminical patterns of religion. Each of these movements influenced the Indian religion in its own way. Primary among these diverse movements were that of Ajivikas, the Jains and the Buddhists. They made their appearance around sixth century B.C. and protested mainly against the system of sacrifice. They advocated that sacrifice was in no way enabling human beings to overcome the fundamental limitations of the *samsara* and human existence.

The Ajivikas accepted the concepts of *samsara* and rebirth as well as death, but they did not accept the doctrine of *karma*. They held that the cosmic principle determined the universe and also every other thing it possessed within it. Therefore, nothing could change the universe and human fate. They rejected the principle of k*arma* and thereby condemned the idea that good karma could influence human fate. The Ajivikas held that even asceticism in one's life was already destined by fate. Consequently, they totally rejected the doctrine of *karma*.

A non-Brahman prince Vardhamana, who was later on known as Mahavira, the founder of Jainism, rejected the concepts of sacrifice and gods that were popularly held important with Brahmanism. The Jains held firmly that the ideas of rebirth and death were good and good *karma* could help bringing change to human bondage. They accepted that *jiva* or self exists in each human being and every kind of material consciousness around it is experienced because of *karma* which goes on creating further *karma* on account of one's daily activities (*karma)*. The only way, they advocated to be free from the whirlpool of the *karma*, was to lead an ascetic's life. The Jains suggested that people could lead a normal life too but they must practise non-violence (*ahimsa*) to prepare for a good future life. When the accumulated *karma* of the past and the present life would be eradicated, the *jiva* would attain freedom and lead an inactive blissful life. The Jains did not believe in the existence of gods, therefore, they totally rejected the idea of sacrifice. As time passed, the Jainism continued to influence people's lives. In India, it is still practised by a good number of people and patronized by the richest class in the society. On account of its early strength and to a considerably continued presence, Jainism has exerted a great influence on the Hindu way of life and Hinduism as well.

Siddhartha Gautama, who founded Buddhism, was a royal prince and belonged to non-Brahman class like Vardhamana. In all Indian history of religion, Buddhism is one of the most significant religious movements. Gautama rejected the concept of sacrifice and the idea of the authority of the *Vedas*. He upheld that personal search to attain freedom from the bondage was the only way to get redeemed from the fetters of *samsara* that cause rebirth and death. Still, Buddhism accepted certain fundamental themes of Brahmanism. In line with it, they accepted the ideas of rebirth, death and *samsara* but wholly rejected the concepts of Brahman or *atman* just as they condemned the idea of sacrifice. Acceptance of certain themes and rejection of the others very strongly influenced the Indian way of life to a considerable extent.

The new lines of thought, which seemed to have been better stated by their founders, were accepted by the people of the Indian sub-continent, for the new ways promised a better way of life. Consequently, Hinduism was confronted with powerful forces that condemned and challenged some of its fundamental themes, which had been popular with the people in the past. In spite of the diverse ideologies recommended by the newly created religious movements in the sixth century B.C., a distinctive feature of Hinduism has been to accept the diversity. As a result, though the above referred religious movements were quite strong, especially for suggesting newer ways of life to get freedom and endless bliss, many of their aspects were gradually accepted and absorbed in a broader way. Consequently, Hindus always respect the founders of the other religions. Perhaps, it was because of Hindu way of liberalism that the followers of the other religions also started accepting some of the old themes popular in Brahmanic period. It is really surprising that a Jain worships Ganesha and a Sikh adores the Shakti or the Goddess Kali as a Hindu does in his every day life. Hinduism has, therefore, an edge on other religions in this respect.

(v) The Growth of Orthodoxy

With the advent of new waves in religious thought, three groups of different followers were distinctly observed within Indian religious arena. These are the Buddhists, the Ajivikas and the Jains about which we have already referred to here above. They totally rejected the *sruti* doctrine (that *Vedas* were divinely revealed). They were taken to be the non-believers (*nastika*). The other religious followers accepted the authority of the *Vedas* and upheld the existence of the Brahman. They were the believers' (*astika*) group of orthodox nature. Since then the term orthodox has often been used while defining Hinduism.

Besides, the acceptance of *varna* (caste) factor in the society was also an important ingredient in the Brahmanic way of life. The caste system, that was later on upheld as a strong orthodox way of life, was primarily the creation of the Aryans, who with their white complexion segregated the indigenous people of India. The white, who were mainly the Aryans, were taken as the superior class, while the darker in complexion, the indigenous ones, were taken to be the lower in status in the society. According to their complexion the divisions of the vocations were also made. The people with the darker complexion were considered *sudras* (lower in class), and were assigned mean jobs. All this paved the way of orthodox Hinduism. To a large extent, it is being followed even today in the Indian sub-continent. In spite of conspicuous recommendations contained in the Constitution of India, the government has not been quite successful in eradicating the caste system.

(vi) The Rise of Hinduism

The above elements, that gradually appeared in the Indian religion from the third millennium B.C. until the sixth century B.C., laid the foundation for the future Indian theological ideals. But as time passed by, more new ideas also cropped up in the period that followed the sixth century. So far most of the theological ideals were carried on orally and it had widely covered various aspects relating to human conduct in general. As man gradually started participating in the duties that brought him gods' company, he also reflected upon individual's conduct for it was important to survive. The great Chinese philosopher Confucius thought in the similar manner a little later. Therefore, now it was time to highlight the theological principles that would influence individual's conduct.

The period between 500 to 200 B.C. is often referred to as the *Sutra* period when various texts were written. These texts contained instructions for the religious acts or the sacrifices and the ceremonies that took place in the household. This literature known as *Sastras* contained instructions for personal conduct. It also contained material relating to the problems of law and statecraft. These *Sastras* covered instructions for all spheres of human conduct. Thus, Hinduism possessed another source of authority in *Sastras,* besides *Sruti* of the earlier *Vedic* period. The *Sutras* and *Sastras* are known as *Smriti* (remembered), which have great authority too but are considered secondary to the *Vedas* as they are conceived to have been revealed.

During the same period, another kind of literature also appeared. It became so popular that it continued prevailing in the subsequent centuries. The two great epics, the *Ramayana* and *Mahabharata,* with their accounts of gods' exploits in human form to establish good and to shun evil, are still immensely popular. These epics, containing the story of gods' fighting on earth to install good (*dharma*), have served throughout Indian history of religion to assure the Hindu that gods come down to the earth when need arises to help humans and their society. The epics have two central figures Rama and Krishna who are deities or *avtaras* (incarnation). They have descended on the earth from the heaven to shun down evil and to uphold the good. Rama is one of the greatest god's incarnations who is the embodiment of ideal human conduct unparalleled in all times. He has since been a great inspiring force in the history of Indian religion. Besides, Krishna, another *avtara* of god and architect of *Bhagavad Gita*, has constantly been an ultimate goal to the Hindu posterity. Thus, the *Ramayana* and the *Mahabharata* have always served as the greatest scriptures of Hinduism. As the torchbearers, they have become sources of ethical commandment and traditional teaching as well as devotion since their creation.

Besides the epics, later on, the *Puranas* have been great sources to teach the ideals and moral principles for the proper conduct of the individual belonging to any profession. The *Puranas*, like the epics, have also served as a primary vehicle for the religious beliefs and worship of the Hindu masses. There are eighteen *Puranas* and numberless local or regional *Puranas* that are found throughout India. The local *Puranas* are usually associated with local temples and tell about gods' exploits. They contain stories about the origin and destruction of the world conveying a sense of the presence of the divine in past and future. Thus, they assure the Hindu that the universe is bound to follow a divine order in future. Therefore, the *Puranas* have also served as a main patron for the rise of devotional Indian religion in the ensuing centuries besides the *Ramanaya* and the *Bhagvad Gita*.

Along with the *Ramanaya, Bhagvad Gita* and the *Puranas* that perpetuated immensely the glory of the Indian religion in varied form, Patanjali's Yoga, during the first century A.D., also contributed a lot in that direction. Yoga is the practice or teaching of great significance in Hinduism. It became clearly perceptible in the post-Upanisadic period though it belonged to the ancient time. There were various factors attached with the *yogic* practices that made it extremely popular. The idea to gain power through meditation and by leading an ascetic way of life, was one of the factors that endeared it to the Hindu masses. The *Yoga* also stressed upon making a distinction between the innate self and the material person. This thought was in line with the *Upanisadic* traditions. Finally, there was an increasing stress upon controlling the body by the absolute self through the *yogic* practices. These factors were so endearing to the Hindu masses that they paved the way for its acceptance widely in Indian religion. The popularity of *yoga* is not limited to the Hindus in India only. It is widely accepted by the people throughout the world.

The *Vedantic* way of attaining *moksha* or to get the final release is also strongly supported by yoga as it has a strong conviction that the individual is required to be unattached by the material world to attain *moksha.* Controlling one's body is the first step in *yogic* practices, which is absolutely imperative in attaining the final release. All that cannot easily be attempted without the help of a *guru* or a trained teacher. Thus, Patanjali's *yogic* contribution towards Hinduism has been great. Most indigenous Indian religions not only appreciated *yoga*, they also involved *yogic* practices as the part of their religious techniques.

One more element is worth reporting to highlight the process of the rise of Hinduism during the centuries under discussion. It is the growing trend on *bhakti* or devotion towards a personal god to attain freedom or *moksha*. The *Vedantic* idea of a non-qualified Brahman is beyond anyone's personal reach through *bhakti* as it does not possess any qualities (*nirguna*) though it is all pervading. Such a Brahman is beyond human thought and therefore not approachable. Gradually, the notions about the deities that were recognized during the Vedic-Brahmanic period were often ignored in the later *Upanisadic* period. These ideas were further ignored during the period when the epics and *Puranas* became popular when certain gods were considered closer to individuals as they often involved themselves with the human society. Since the gods displayed their love towards the individual and intervened with the human affairs to redeem man from the evil, human attention and love towards them was quite natural. Therefore, devotion to the gods was recognized as an easy and a sure process to attain *moksha.* Thus, growing emphasis on *bhakti* brought changes in the approaches towards the former *Upanisadic* concept of Brahman. Now there is a reference to a Brahman in a personalized manner. It is the cause of existence and the source of human self. Therefore, Brahman possesses qualities and as such knowable and approachable as well. Gradually, this kind of thinking laid the foundation for theistic devotional worship within the Vedic-Brahmanic heritage.

This sort of belief gets an accelerated impetus during the time of the epics when gods descend on the earth, perform great adventures and demonstrate a loving concern towards mankind for the maintenance of *dharma* (truth). It has also been confirmed by the literature that these beings are ultimately divine. Krishna as an *avtar* (incarnation) of Vishnu asserts in the *Bhgavad Gita*:

> अजोऽपि सन्नव्ययात्मा भूतानामीश्वरोऽपि सन्।।
> प्रकृतिं स्वामधिष्ठाय सम्भवाम्यात्ममायया।।६।।
> **Though I am unborn, of changeless nature**
> **and Lord of beings, yet subjugating My Prakriti,**
> **I come into being by My own Maya.** (Ch.4.6)*

Sri Krishna continues further,

> **परित्राणाय साधूनां विनाशाय च दुष्कृताम् ।।**
> **धर्मसंस्थापनार्थाय संभावामि युगे युगे ।।८।।**
> **In order to protect the good,**
> **to destroy the doers of evil,**
> **to ensure the triumph of righteousness,**
> **in every age I am born.** (Ch.4.8)

It means that God comes to the earth time and again for the destruction of evil and wicked, and for the protection and the establishment of good and righteousness. With this kind of belief in vogue, the idea of a personal Brahman was firmly established in the Indian religion. Hinduism was now equipped to meet the different religious desires of the greater majority of the Hindu population even if a few diverse movements had already taken place on account of its certain unacceptable themes to them.

(vii) Classical Hinduism

It was during the Sutra period, which roughly began a little before the start of the first century A.D., certain peculiarities were seen between various schools of thought and practices in Indian religion. During these early years, six schools of Indian philosophical thought having a theological bearing evolved distinctly. These were Nyaya, Vaisesika, Samkhya, Yoga, Mimansa and Vedanta. Each of these schools was equally well founded as a pathfinder to *moksha*, therefore, classified as an orthodox (*astika*) school. Besides these schools, two other schools of thought, Buddhism and Jainism, were known as the heterodox (*nastika*) schools. They did not believe in Brahman or *moksha*. These two heterodox schools did believe in the liberation of the self but with a different approach and destination.

In view of our discussion on the orthodox system of theological thought, I would like to concentrate more on the Vedanta school as most of the other orthodox schools are influenced mainly by it (Vedanta) in this way or the other. Besides, it is the only school of thought, which has influenced most of the Indian masses in their way of life and religious practices. It would not be untrue to state that it is Vedanta that has served predominantly as a religious torchbearer to the Hindu masses. In fact, within Vedanta, three systems of thought have mostly influenced the Hindu way of life since long. I would like to discuss them separately in brief at this juncture to enable the believer to know that how without going into the variety of the system he or she is involved with either of it consciously or unknowingly.

One of the strong missionaries of the Vedanta system of thought, *Samkara* during 800 A.D., claimed that 'each human being consists of a self, which as an entity is related to, in some manner, with the Ultimate Person, Brahman.' He also claimed that this human self, the *atman*, is independent of the physical body. It is also separate from the mental or the psychic aspect of the individual. It is a great error to identify the self with the body or the mind. That kind of understanding of the self leads it to ignorance, which is the source of every kind of human problem. The cause of rebirth and death is ignorance. Therefore, experiencing *samsara* and pain is caused on account of man's ignorance, which is also the cause of confusion. It is simply on account of ignorance that individual confuses the empirical with the Ultimate Real. It is the knowledge of Brahman that will destroy ignorance. The only Real is Brahman that is without limitation. The empirical world, experienced through one's senses, is devoid of the qualities that Brahman possesses.

In fact, the world of experience is Maya, creative power of Brahman. As long as an individual is attached to the domain of Maya, he/she cannot know the qualityless Brahman. Only those attain *moksha* who possess the right knowledge and are spiritually disciplined. Right knowledge can be obtained through meditation upon the *Upanisadic* text. Thus, the individual (*ascetic*) who has renounced the world and is ready to follow the *yogic* discipline can attain the right knowledge. The right knowledge gained through meditation is the knowledge that human self starts identifying itself with the Ultimate Self or Brahman. That means the *atman* or the innate self finally meets Brahman. It is also understood as Samkara's absolute non-dualism (*Advaita*). This is how Samkara perceived the teaching of the *Upanisads*.

The second intellectual thinker within the *Vedantic* system after Samkara in the eleventh century was Ramanujam. He acknowledged the reality of the world, the individual and the Brahman. Ramanujam conceives Brahman as primary, while the individual selves and the physical world are dependent upon Brahman. Although the self comes from Brahman, it remains a separate and discrete entity. Ramanujam's belief of this sort is known as a qualified non-dualism (*Visista Advaita*). It means the unified Brahman is manifesting itself both as matter and selves. An individual can attain *moksha* by obtaining the knowledge of Brahman. That knowledge can come through meditation, devotion and by receiving the divine grace of Brahman. By divine grace, Ramanujam means all those qualities that Brahman possesses. Brahman will respond favourably to the self only when it acquires those qualities. Only that self, that can develop a separate and blissful relationship with Brahman, can get redeemed from the *samsara*. That is the only way to be liberated from the rebirth and death, according to Ramanujam.

There was one more champion of *Vedantic* thought during the thirteenth century. He is known as Madhavacharya who conceives that Brahman, the human self and the world possess eternal permanency. Thus, for Madhava reality is of a dualistic (*Dvaita*) nature. Clarifying the nature of the human self and the world, he states that although the self and the world are permanent, they are dependent on Brahman. Perhaps Madhava was highly influenced by *Bhagavata Purana*, therefore, he emphasized the importance of Brahman's role in controlling the world as well as all the selves.

Madhava argues that Brahman and Vishnu are one. Therefore, one who is a devotee of Vishnu or Krishna who is deemed to be an *avtar* of Vishnu, is also a devotee of Brahman. Vishnu is the only power in the world that can help release a human self (leading a pure life) from the bondage of the *samsara*. The individuals, who don't lead a pure life, are not capable to receive Brahman's grace. Neither they can ever attain *moksha*. Thus, *Vedanta* laid the foundation of Hindu religious thought implicit with the idea of devotion.

Although there is a great variety of thoughts between the *Vedantic* intellectual theologians, they all uphold the *sruti* of the *Vedas*. Thus, they endorse the existence of Brahman, and accept that the human self is either identical or has a close relationship with the Ultimate Brahman. They also maintain that *moksha* is also possible and the self can be redeemed from rebirth and death as well as from the bondage of the *samsara*.

The centuries, that followed Madhava, witnessed more formal theological developments connected with the *Vedanta*. Different ways to attain *moksha* were discovered during this period to help man get redeemed from the bondage of the world. As a result of formal reflection and inquiry, different procedures became firmly fixed in the Hindu mind. Besides the Indian religious thought and practice, these paths got a great support of and approval by many *Vedantic* thinkers of that period. Consequently, these paths, which were threefold, obtained a recognized status among the Hindu masses and became essential aspects of Hinduism. These were: (i) *The way of action* (*karma*) or deeds which required an individual to perform cultic sacrifices and discharge social obligations in his life as a part of his *dharma*. It was a kind of extension of the Vedantic-Brahmanical ideology. (ii) *The way of knowledge* (*jnana*). It involved the individual to withdraw from usual social activities and required discipline of mind and body to reach the true selfhood. This kind of thinking received its support from Samkara's views. (iii) *The way of devotion* (*bhakti*). Both Ramanujam and Madhavacharya strongly believed that devotion and love for a personal God were supreme. It was a sure and easy way to attain *moksha* and understand Brahman. But it has never been necessary to follow only one path out of the three. Most Hindus inadvertently indulge with some aspects of the three in their personal lives. One of the best examples in this respect is that of Sri Ramakrishna, who started his devotional journey through the worship of a personal God or Goddess Kali, but after meeting his guru Totapuri, all his efforts were diverted towards the unqualified (*nirakar*) Brahman.

(viii) Prevalence of Theism

It is almost past one thousand years that the essential feature of Hinduism and of the majority of the Hindus has been to follow the path of devotion. God with different Hindu names including the goddesses, who possess creative powers, have been the centre of devotion and worship of the millions of people in India. This sort of theistic ideology, which is a departure from Samkara's *Advitavad*, has gained much popularity with the people of India after Ramanujam. The *bhakti marg* or the devotional path of the Hindu religion focuses mainly on the worship of some aspect of the great gods like Vishnu or Shiva. We have already discussed how the *Puranas* and the *Bhagavad Gita* served in promoting the devotional way to enable the individual to come close to the gods and goddesses.

Besides these texts, there are local or regional *Puranas* which have served a lot in popularizing the *bhakti marg* and developing understanding among the general masses about the gods and their relationship with man. The regional *Puranas*, in fact, became more popular on account of people's interest in listening to the stories of gods' adventures, presented to the masses through dance, drama or story telling. In this manner the great Hindu gods are localized and accepted for regular worship. As a result of intense love of men for the gods or the goddesses and in return gods' love, humans attaining *moksha* has never been thought difficult.

The devotional leadership of the theistic nature after Ramanujam was furnished by a number of exceptional men and women who by their religious and devotional practices influenced a lot of Indian masses. Among them, one of the most notables is Ramananda, who during the beginning of the fifteenth century convinced the people of his immense love for Rama, the incarnate of Vishnu. Another important name of a great devotee of god is Caitanya Mahaprabhu. During the beginning of the sixteenth century, he unfolded his message of great love for god to all castes and stressed that Krishna, who was Vishnu's incarnation, should be worshiped. In that list of the great devotees one more name, Tulsidas, is worth mentioning at this point, though there are other names too. Tulsidas, who later on out of reverence and love, was known as the saint Tulsidas, during the middle of the sixteenth century (1532-1623), wrote in Hindi language the story of Rama and furnished it with his immense emotional love and devotion for Him. The epic *Ramayana* renamed by Tulsidas as *Ramcaritmanas*, presented to the Indian masses through drama and song since then, has proved a great promoter of the *bhakti* movement in the modern times. When the *bhakti* movement was in its full swing in the northern India and also extended considerably to the east and the south of the country, foreign invaders attacked India from the north and brought with them their religion which they forced on the people of the sub-continent. But Hinduism by then had been so firmly rooted in the Indian soil that in spite of the recurrent invasions and conversions, it survived. Not only that, there were reactions against such conversion. These reactions can be witnessed in different forms.

(ix) Reactions against other Religions

During the eleventh century, Muslim invaders, primarily from Afghanistan, began their intrusion into the north India. By the first half of the thirteenth century, Muslim rule began establishing itself in the country. Within another three hundred years, Muslim rule extend over almost the entire subcontinent. Leaving a few Rajput states and some parts of the south, most of India was under the Muslim rule. It was quite natural that some Indians on account of various reasons would convert to Islam. It also happened during the British regime after the Moghul Empire vanished that some Indians were converted into Christianity. But the great majority of the Hindus remained within their framework. They always tried to express their religious traditions through certain rituals, devotion and love and opposed in principle the invaders' religious impositions. Among the people who demonstrated their great concern towards the Indian theological principles and practices and exhibited their profound love for God were those of Kabir and Guru Nanak. During the late fifteenth and early sixteenth centuries, they both attracted a great majority of people by their devotional feats and songs and opposed the religious conversions that were in vogue during that time.

Kabir's teachings played the role of a spiritual teacher or *guru* in the individual's spiritual progress. It was also an ancient tradition within the Indian religion. Nanak's teachings concentrated upon the worship of one God, the "True Name" to whom the many Hindu gods bear witness. He accepted the doctrine of *karma* and *moksha* and rejected the caste differences as well as the worship of images. But he approved many sorts of religious ceremonies that were dearly loved by the Indian masses.

(x) Modern Hinduism

With the passage of time and many new movements cropping

up since the formalization of Hinduism almost a thousand years before, many fresh traditions crept into the religious system. The stress on sacrifice gradually receded with the advent of the nineteenth century, but certain social customs like burning a widow alive at the occasion of the death of her husband and accepting big dowry during the event of a Hindu marriage came in vogue. The dowry system, that originated sometimes during the eighteenth century or even earlier, gradually got distorted on account of the greedy bridegroom's parents. Perhaps, its start must have been with a clear good intention but as times passed on, the system gathered evil intentions. So was the case of burning a woman alive with the pyre of her dead husband. Many such social customs and rituals became unbearable to the people, especially the poor.

One of the champion reformers, who brought some solace to the sick social traditions in India during the late eighteenth century, was Ram Mohan Roy, who with his untiring efforts challenged the prevalent social evils and initiated 'reform movements' in India. Ram Mohan Roy's *Brahmo Samaj*, Swami Dayanand's *Arya Samaj* and Sri Ramakrishna's *Ram Krishna Mission* backed by Swami Vivekananda's untiring efforts are the best examples of social reforms during nineteenth and twentieth centuries. Names of Sri Aurobondo and Dr Sarvepalli Radhakrishnan must not be forgotten to mention at this point. During the late nineteenth and twentieth centuries, they influenced the Hindu society immensely. Sri Aurobindo maintained that the ultimate truth of existence could only be attained from the mystic vision that one could experience through pious devotion and meditation. Dr. Radhakrishnan, through his rich and abundant philosophical writings, clarified many of the ambiguous and difficult concepts of Hinduism and provided convincing lucidity to make their meaning clear. In the second half of the twentieth century, Mohan Das Karamchand Gandhi caught the attention of the Westerners and created their interest to understand Hinduism closely.

Although the efforts of the above mentioned intellectuals of India are more than praiseworthy as far as reforms are concerned in Hinduism, their striving is more palatable and perceptible to the educated elite to a great extent. Most of the uneducated masses have their own way and procedure to know and practise Hinduism. They know it well only through the regional *Puranas* and the epics. Besides, the age-old traditions, which provide them a sense of the divine in this world and hereafter, are the best propagators of the old religion. A pious Hindu, belonging to any profession or social class, knows it well that he can reach the divine by devotion, constant prayers and meditation and *moksha* can be attained.

Modern Hinduism is not a sum total of all the previous religious beliefs. It includes almost all and every way of life that promises and helps attaining *moksha*. It includes an ascetic way of life, which is a homeless wandering in the quest of Brahman. It includes visiting the holy places (*four dhams*) and performing the necessary religious rituals at those sacred places. Almost every pious Hindu family has a small shrine in his/her house, where he/she performs formal or informal worship each day in the quest of God or *moksha*. There are those Hindus too for whom religion is a secondary matter. Yet these people do have a sense of a religious life of which they are always a part. They may not formally worship any gods, but they do participate in the social rites that have been approved by the religious canons. Hinduism in that sense is a great religion, though some may not take it to be a religion. What shall be its future shape no one knows but whatever form it possesses today, it is certainly great. Its age-old beliefs and traditions that gave it a great start cannot be condemned totally. Some of them would have been outwitted by the passage of time (so is the case with other religions too), but many of them still stand upright as a testimony that great truth is implicit with them.

Chapter Two

How Beliefs Emanated

The Aryan Dharma

If we trace the history of Indian religion, we find that the old term for religion in India was *Arya dharma*. Dharma really meant something more than religion. Its root meaning is 'to hold together.' It is the law of the inner being. It is an ethical concept, which includes the moral code, righteousness and entire field of man's duties as well as responsibilities. *Arya dharma*, to my belief and knowledge, includes all the faiths, Vedic and non-Vedic, that instituted in India. The Buddhists and Jains used this term too. Thus, all those faiths which originated from the Vedantic ideology and which acknowledged the general authority of the *Vedas* belonged to the Vedic dharma. The Buddhists and Jains who refused to accept the Vedic authority were also very much influenced by the Vedic ideology. Although they refuted a few aspects of the Vedic traditions, most of the remaining aspects that flourished with these two non-Vedic religions, were taken from the Vedic traditions. For example, the Buddhists rejected the idea of sacrifice and refuted the authority of the gods. But they accepted the importance of the moral code as they thought that it was necessary to lead a happy life. They also believed that it would help man attain freedom and happiness and show him the right path, which would provide him satisfaction. Therefore, though Buddhism and Jainism are not considered as Vedic religions, they cannot be totally excluded from it, as basically they accepted many of their ideological aspects. Besides, rejecting someone's ideology is not a promise for excluding its influence on the one who rejects it. It is on the ground that the basic idea that had belonged to someone else has simply either been rejected or amended before acceptance. Therefore, if both these non-Vedic faiths cannot be included within the Vedic dharma, they cannot be excluded from it.

The entire theme of the *Bhagavad Gita* is rooted with the idea of fulfilling one's duty, which is the highest code of conduct for man in this life. Similarly, Buddha and Mahaveera both stressed the importance of a code of conduct that would lead man to attain *nirvana*, a term used to denote *moksha* by the Buddhists and the Jains. Thus, man's search for truth, which initially began with the awesome wonders of the nature, did not finish with the worshipping the animals or pleasing the gods with sacrifices. It went much further and culminated into a point that seemed to be a kind of pinnacle if not the end point. What is truth? What is its nature? These are the highest points of man's reflections in the field of philosophy and religion. Although man has taken different paths and enormous time to reach the current stage of perception and evaluating, it cannot be denied that the direction of the process has been quite correct to a large extent. Let us start digging out progressively from the past how Hindu beliefs originated and how ultimately they came under one umbrella, known as Hinduism.

Inadequate Interpretations

Hinduism as a religion has come to be called by Westerners as a complex product of various cults and beliefs put together within a common social framework, called caste system. It procured its distinctive form in the period that ensued the *Upanishads* when the importance of favourite gods as objects of devotion increased. In fact, it was a trend, which grew as a result of blending the popular beliefs nurtured during the growth of the Vedic and Brahmanical religious traditions some of which rooted from the time of Indus Valley Civilization.

It is really so difficult to define Hinduism in a few words.

Once when I was invited to deliver a short lecture in the Humanities Department of Ohio University, at Ohio, USA during 1980s, someone put a question to me, 'What is Hinduism?' Until then although being a Hindu, I had never thought that it would be so difficult to answer that question. I had to scratch my mind many times before I answered the question. At the end of my talk, I felt within myself a bit disturbed as I felt that I was inadequate about it, though the students, who were ignorant about the subject, seemed contented. As a faith, Hinduism may seem to be vague because it is many-sided, all things to all men. It is, therefore, hardly possible to define it. In its present form and even in the past, it embraces many beliefs and practices, many of which are opposed to or contradictory to each other. Pt. Jawaharlal Nehru, in his book *Discovery of India*, reflecting about Hinduism, states that, 'its essential spirit seems to be to live and let live' Quoting Mahatma Gandhi, Nehru unfolded his views in the following lines: 'If I were asked to define the Hindu creed, I should simply say: "Search after truth through non-violent means. A man may not believe in God and still call himself a Hindu. Hinduism is a relentless pursuit after truth. Truth is God. Denial of God we have known. Denial of truth we have not known." Thus, Hinduism can be defined, as a religion of truth only and no more confusing explanations about it would be justified.

The Process of Inception

Prior to the discovery of the Indus Valley Civilization, the *Vedas* were supposed to be the earliest records of Indian cultural, religious and philosophical practices. In fact, there has been a great dispute to assertion the chronology of the *Vedic* period. Western scholars think that the beginnings of *Vedic* literature go back to 2000 B.C. or even 2500 B.C. While Indian scholars think it to be much earlier. Probably, they do so as they wish to enhance the importance of their ancient culture. But even if we take it to be starting from 2500 B.C., we come very close to the Mohenjo-Daro period. Whatever the exact date of the creation of the Indian culture and religious history may be, it is quite likely that *Vedas* existed earlier than that of the Greece or even Israel. The Vedic literature represents some of the finest documents of human mind that reflected on the nature of the world, God and human soul. It tried to find out what is the ultimate nature of Reality. Although all that was simply an outcome of the Aryans' deep mental reflections, it is certainly an excellent record of highly advanced minds that intellectually and wisely contemplated on the difficult issues that are still obscure and difficult to define. Max Muller has summarized it in few words only. He called it: 'the first word spoken by the Aryan man.'

In this chapter, I desire to discern what beliefs and practices the Aryans and later intellectuals possessed and practised and how all that enhanced the cause of Hinduism in future. I also wish to throw some light on how these beliefs cropped up. If a belief doesn't come out true with the passage of time, it is simply a belief and not the truth. The pragmatic approach supports this idea too. But it is really so unfortunate that so far many beliefs like 'the existence of the Ultimate, the existence of *atman* or self in the physical body, and whether it can identify itself with Brahman' are still beliefs and need to be tested. Most of the Hindus and many people in different parts of the world accept those beliefs. But how far all these notions or beliefs can be tested logically, cannot be stated. A belief will remain a belief only even if a great number of people accept it as a truth. However, beliefs like gods' coming to the earth in human form to intervene in man's affairs, especially to eradicate the evil and to help humans follow the good, can be accepted simply on the basis that it certainly has a far reaching impact on the human mind and conduct.

Well, when the Aryans entered the rich land of India, they brought with them their ideas and elaborated them in this land. It is not the beliefs and practices that merely influenced the people of India when the Aryans entered the country. Much more than that, it was their style, the eloquence, the beauty of the phrases and sentences contained in the *Vedas* that left lasting effect on the people. It is not the metaphysics or the description of the ritualistic practices including usefulness and necessity of sacrifice that are so impressive. It is the human mind and its way of reflecting on the obscure and confusing human issues that is more important. Thus, the procedure of the wise men of that time was so impressive that people started believing in it. In fact, it is a matter of great wonder and significance that what manner of men and women they were who gave shape to all those bright ideas and lovely fancies. Perhaps, it was also their creation that the *Vedas* contain the revealed knowledge. Why most people started believing in it, is a matter of get wonder! It cannot be testified by any kind of research now, as the passage of time has been so immense since then. It is also true about the world's other religions, whose holy books are known to have been revealed.

Religion is a matter of faith only and often there is no room for logic. Therefore, we drop the issue of testing the hypothesis 'whether the *Vedas* are a revealed knowledge'. But we cannot deny that they certainly contain immensely splendid wisdom that can help us transcending the ordinary human plain and elevate us to most lofty heights beyond human imagination. No great temples are reported to have been built by the Aryans during the period of the *Vedas*. The life they led was immensely simple, happy and full of zest. Perhaps, they paid little attention to the soul but vaguely they believed in some kind of existence after death. The Vedic literature, created out of a happy go life, contains hymns, prayers, certain rituals for sacrifice to please the nature-gods who were supposed to have possessed power and often interfered in man's day to day life. Of course, nature plays an important role in men's lives. It is, therefore, highly revered in many ways and forms. So was the case during ancient times when the Aryan civilization started to grow.

Gradually, after a lapse of time, the conception of God or Brahman appeared in the Aryans' mind. They desired to see someone above all the smaller gods—someone who was still stronger and would reflect unity with all that plurality. Therefore, the creation or let us say the conception of all the different kinds of gods, like Indra, Sun, Varuna and others was culminated in one whole, Brahman. Thus, with the passage of time monotheism turned into monism. As a result of man's awe towards the Nature and its mysterious objects, all these developments must have taken place during hundreds of years.

Outcome of Wonder

Hinduism includes many different and even contradictory beliefs. In spite of the great regional and sectarian variations of religious beliefs, there are certain main characteristics that typically belong to Hinduism. During the course of time as human civilization started developing and man started devising ways and means to live happily, he suddenly realized that death was also a fact of life. Every living entity that was born must die also. This realization must have created a kind of fear and dissatisfaction in the minds of the people who were trying very hard to improve their lot by applying their minds to grow food and to collect information about eatable items. Food was always a great necessity not only to sustain the body but also as a pastime for it interestingly fills the gaps of time when man has nothing to do for him. But the discovery of the fact that man would die also, landed him in a dungeon of dilemma, fear and despair.

Gradually, he must have started finding ways to be away from death. Years must have passed in that quest until he started wondering and fearing the Nature's unusual behaviour. It was so difficult to know who sent rain and how clouds formed. With that the lightening must have caused a strange fear in his mind. The sun also reflected its heat regularly. As years passed on, the heat of the sun must have appeared to him big, soothing and worthy of inflicting harm too. Such attributes for a natural object that man could neither touch, or reach, nor stop it from rising from the east, must have been the cause of awe. Thus, the story of reckoning the unusual natural objects as gods must have begun. These gods were unusually powerful, and therefore, it was natural to reckon them as supernatural. So he began to believe that Agni, Indra, Varuna, Rudra and Surya were gods. Agni controlled the life force, of fire and sacrifice; Indra was taken to be the god of war and storm; Varuna was the god of sky, day and night; and Rudra was the god of mountains. The Sun or Surya was described as the 'Eye of Varuna.' These heavenly bodies, which were unusually mighty, were gradually taken to be secondary when man started thinking all of a sudden that there should have been a greater entity responsible for creating and controlling them all. He named that entity, Brahman. We have already reflected on it briefly a little while ago.

No body knows how much time man would have taken to conclude it finally, but this kind of thought must have been awesome and alarming as well. I think it must have also been pacifying, as for long man was trying to discover some kind of unity to his scattered ideas he believed true. This creator with the passage of time was known Brahman. Then the idea of a preserver also cropped up in man's mind. Vishnu was the God man named as the Preserver and Controller of human life. Then he thought of another God who would be responsible to destroy the world if need arises on account of man's unwarranted conduct. He named him Shiva.

It is really surprising that while man identified each god as the source of some kind of heavenly benediction, he associated a goddess with him. As this thought emerged, he devised two names, Sarasvati and Lakshmi. The former was taken to be the Goddess of Knowledge and Truth, and the later the Goddess of fortune, wealth and beauty. Sarasvati was gradually associated with Brahma, a third equally powerful god like Shiva and Vishnu. With the passage of time the three Gods, Brahma, Vishnu and Mahesh (Shiva) created Shakti, the Goddess of Great power. She was created as the gods wanted to bring to an end one of the deadliest demons who had acquired strange boons from Brahma and Shiva. As a result of acquiring unusual boons from the Highest Gods, the demon became invincible. No one could kill him but some one like Shakti or Kali. Thus, the three supreme gods to kiil the invincible demon created Shakti.

When Doctrines Matured

These beliefs were gradually cemented as a result of repeatedly listening to the popular tales contained in the great epics, the basis of the vast and colorful Indian mythology. One of these epics, the *Mahabharata*, contains within it the most fascinating spiritual poem of the Bhagavad Gita. The Gita is a dialogue between God Krishna (incarnation of Vishnu) and Arjuna, one of the five Pandava princes involved in fighting against the Kauravas. Arjuna is forced to combat his own kinsmen in the great family war. It forms the main story of *Mahabharata*.

Though Krishna is an *avtar* (incarnation), he acts as Arjuna's charioteer. He drives the chariot right between the two armies. In that dramatic setting of the battlefield, he starts to reveal to Arjuna the most profound truths about Hinduism. As Krishna speaks, the realistic background of the war between the two families declines. It becomes clear that the battle of Arjuna is the spiritual battle of human nature. It is a battle of the warrior in search of enlightenment. When Arjuna is full of despair and refuses to fight, Krishna himself advises him to fight and says:

> तस्मादज्ञानसंभूतं हृत्स्थं ज्ञानासिनात्मनः ।।
> छित्त्वैनं संशयं योगमातिष्ठोत्तिष्ठ भारत ।।४२।।
> **Therefore, with the sword of wisdom**
> **Cut off this doubt in your heart;**
> **follow the path of selfless**
> **action; stand up, Arjuna!** (4. 42)

It is the basis of Krishna's spiritual instruction that the idea of multiple of all things and events around us are but different manifestations of the same Ultimate Reality. It is also one of the potent ideas of Hinduism. This reality known as Brahman is the unifying idea that gives Hinduism its essential character, although it reckons the worshipping of numerous gods and goddesses. Brahman, the Ultimate Reality, is taken to be the soul or inner essence of all things. It is infinite and beyond all concepts. It cannot be understood by the intellect. It can also not be described in words. Brahman is beginningless. It is supreme and beyond what is and beyond what is not. It cannot be comprehended, as it is a Supreme Soul. It is unlimited, unborn and not to be reasoned about. It is unthinkable etc.

While trying to dispel Arjuna's despair further, Krishna explains to him:

यो मामजमनादिं च वेत्ति लोकमहेश्वरम् ॥
असंमूढः स मर्त्येषु सर्वपापैः प्रमुच्यते ॥३॥
Whoever knows me as the Unborn,
the Beginningless, the great Lord
of all worlds—he alone sees
truly and is free from all harm. (*Gita*, Ch.10.3)

Yet, Arjuna's dismay does not diminish and he still refuses to fight his kinsmen. Then the Blessed Lord tells him:

हन्त ने कथयिष्यामि दिव्या ह्यात्मविभूतयः ॥
प्राधान्य कुरुश्रेष्ठ नास्त्यन्तो विस्तरस्य मे ॥१९॥
All right Arjuna: I will tell you
a few of my manifestations,
the most glorious ones; for infinite
are the forms in which I appear. (Ch.10.19)

The Lord continues:

अहमात्मा गुडाकेश सर्वभूताशयस्थितः ॥
अहमादिश्च मध्यं च भूतानामन्त एव च ॥२०॥
I am the Self, Arjuna,
seated in the heart of all beings;
I am the beginning and life span
of beings, and their end as well. (Ch.10.20)

In spite of the fact that no one can explain Brahman in one word, as he is undeniable, unthinkable, unborn and unlimited, people want to talk about this reality. The numerous Hindu sages have often pictured Brhaman as divine and talk about it in mythological language. At times, they have also stated that the various aspects of the Divine are the names of the various gods that are worshiped by the Hindus. But the scriptures make it absolutely clear that all these gods are simply the reflections of the one Ultimate Reality. Thus, Brahman is the source of all the gods, of every thing seen or unseen. The Gita has implanted the belief about Brahman very strongly. Even after almost four to five thousand years when the *Mahabharata* (referring to the great war between the Kauravs and the Pandavas) took place and the Gita was narrated or sung by Krishna, most Hindus strongly hold **Brahman** as the only Ultimate in this *samsara*.

With the conception of Brahman, man must have desired to confirm his views about the existence of Brahman. Nothing could have been better than to conceive Brahman through the self, as it (self) is the only agent that can describe it possessing a form or no form. Unless the self is also equivalent to Brahman in some way, it would not perceive or comprehend Brahman. Perhaps, that made the idea of *atman* originate. They defined that human soul or *atman* is 'the manifestation of Brahman. Finally, they held that the idea that *atman* and Brahman, the individual and the Ultimate Reality, are one. It is also the essence of the *Upanishads*.

> **That which is the finest essence—this whole world has that as its soul. That is—Reality. That is Atman. That art thou.** (Brihad-aranyaka Upanishad, 4.3.21)

The basic theme in Hindu mythology is the creation of the world by God's sacrifice or desire. This kind of creative activity of Divine is known *lila* or the play of God. Brahman is the great magician who transforms himself into the world. He performs this sort of deed with his magical creative power. This creative power of Brahman is known as *maya*, which has been understood and perceived in different ways. It signifies one of the most important terms in Indian philosophy. Besides conceiving it as the power of Brahman, it has also been taken to signify the psychological state of a person under the spell of the magic play. So far as one confuses the innumerable forms of the *divine lila* with reality, without understanding the unity of Brahman, one remains under the spell of *maya*.

In fact, *maya* does not mean that the world is an illusion, which is mostly stated incorrectly. The illusion simply lies in a person's point of view when he/she conceives that the shapes, structures and events around him/her are realities of Nature. *Maya* is the illusion of taking these concepts for reality. It is just like confusing the map with the territory. The world of *maya* is ever changing. The Hindu belief about Nature is that all forms are relative and ever changing. Gautam Buddha around sixth century BC had rightly conceived that the world is transient and ever changing.

If you don't conceive *maya* as a divine *lila*, you simply misjudge it. As a result, you are unable to perceive the unity lying behind it. So man acts under its spell and acts wrongly for his basic understanding of the world based on illusion. The idea, that man should conceive the world in its real sense, led to originate the theory of *karma.* The meaning of *karma,* like that of *maya,* has also been misunderstood and brought down from its original cosmic level to human level. When Arjuna (referring to Gita) is confused and refuses to fight (act) standing in the middle of the battlefield, Sri Krishna explains to him why must he fight. As long as our view of the world, like Arjuna, is fragmented, so long we are under the spell of *maya* and cannot act independently. We are bound by *karma.* We can only be free from the bond of *karma* when we realize the unity and harmony in all nature and acts accordingly.

Thus, if one wants to be free from the spell of *maya,* one must break the bonds of *karma.* If once right understanding of the world were obtained, one would not act erroneously. By breaking the bonds of *karma* means to realize that all the phenomena one perceives with one's senses is part of the same reality. It also means that everything, including one's own self, is Brahman only. To conceive it something else is illusory. How these notions matured with the passage of time is not known. It cannot be really known now for lot of time has gone by since then. But as soon as man realized clearly that everything perishes with the passage of time, he conceived the idea that the whole world was illusory. That led him to contemplate to find a way to be free from the spell of *maya* or illusion. The idea of rebirth must have been bothering him since long. Once when it was believed that one who is born must die, he would have started thinking on the track how to stop taking birth again.

Although it is a biological consequence that a child takes birth, but giving up every thing in the hands of Brahman, conceiving the whole world as illusory and a play of Brahman, man must have thought on the ways and means that would help him perceive the world in its right perspective. It was long before Gautama Buddha and Mahaveera that the Vedic-Brahmanic religion provided the idea that the world was illusory and it was the pure Self or *atman* that could dissolve or repel the illusion by meeting Brahman. That meeting could take place only when the *atman* would transcend itself to the realm of Brahman. Thus, the meeting of the Self with Brahman was taken to be the final journey of man. They called it *moksha* or the liberated state of the Self. It is the essence of Hinduism.

All other branches of religion, which sprang up as a reaction against the strict ritualistic traditions contained in Hinduism, try to explain that ultimate aim of each individual must be to get rid of the illusory or the transient world and attain liberation or *moksha*. Liberation is the only state of bliss. All other states are implicit with pain and suffering.

Hinduism and its off shoots simply differ on their approaches (ways) to reach that final stage of liberation, but in principle Buddhism, Jainism and Sikhism all agree that man can attain final liberation. I would not like to go into the details what Buddhism and Jainism hold about the ways and procedures to attain liberation (*nirvana*) or *moksha*, for my efforts in this small treatise are limited to Hinduism. I shall, therefore, like to explain what Hinduism holds about the ways of liberation.

Varied Ways to Liberation

Although Hinduism has been quite dogmatic about its certain rituals for long, it has never been so conservative in discovering varied ways to attain liberation. There lies its strength. It is a highly liberal religion on many counts. It holds that there are countless ways to reach a liberated state. It provides different rituals, concepts and spiritual exercises to get different modes of awareness. Although many of these concepts and practices may be contradictory, it does not affect the Hindu mind at all. For each Hindu knows that Brahman is beyond concepts and images, so he accepts every procedure that promises transporting the self to the realm of Brahman. It is from this kind of attitude that tolerance and inconclusiveness is implicit with Hinduism.

Vedanta, one of the most intellectual schools of philosophy in Hinduism, is based on the *Upanishads*. It emphasizes that Brahman is non-personal and is free from any mythological content. In spite of its high intellectual level, the Vedantic way of liberation is very different from most of the Western philosophical approaches. The Vedantins recommend daily meditation and different kinds of spiritual exercises so that man can have union with Brahman. We have already discussed Samkara's approach in the previous chapter in this respect and tried to define the Undeniable Brahman. Besides Samkara, the approaches of Ramanujam and Madhava have also been discussed in this respect in the previous chapter. These ways would clearly indicate to the reader how within the Vedanta different approaches exist to attain liberation or meet Brahman.

In fact, the idea that rebirth and death are the sources of all pain in human life, must have led the wise Aryans to think and find out how to be liberated from these unwanted painful stages of life. It is really so difficult to know how man conceived the idea of rebirth or *transmigration*. But it seems to have worked as an originator of the concept of liberation. If rebirth and death are definite and are in continuous process, ways to break away from that continuity could be thought of. Therefore, the idea of liberation must have been originated as a consequence to consisting the belief in transmigration. Not only Hinduism but also almost all the offshoots of the religion hold that rebirth is a reality as well as the source of misery. Therefore, the Vedantins recommended the ways, which, though difficult, promise to reach the final goal of life, i.e. liberation.

Another important method of liberation that exists with in the boundaries of Hinduism is that of *yoga*. *Yoga* simply means 'joining'. It refers to the joining of the individual soul to Brahman. There are several approaches within *yoga* that include basic physical training and various mental disciplines intended for people of different types and different spiritual levels.

The most popular way for an ordinary Hindu has been to approach the divine by worshiping him/her as a personal god or a goddess. There are hundreds of deities that manifest in a number of ways. We have already indicated the three most revered and worshiped deities— Shiva, Vishnu and Brahma. Later on, one more deity added to the list is the Divine Mother, Kali. Shiva is one of the oldest Indian gods who can assume many forms. His most celebrated appearance is that of *Natraj*, the greatest Dancer. Since He is the Cosmic Dancer, Shiva is the god of creation as well as destruction. It is through His endless dance and rhythm that He sustains the universe. There are stories contained in the scriptures how Shiva, time to time, out of compassion and kindness has bestowed boons to His ardent devotees making them invincible. Some of the devotees, who are demons too, with the passage of time, start going out of the way and threaten the gods and angels in the heaven. It is at such occasions and many other times too when the gods and angels are imperiled by the demon devotee, the goddess Shakti comes to the rescue of the gods and restores the heaven for them by killing the demons.

Lord Vishnu, Who is supposed to be the supreme god among the three, appears in different forms and often incarnates in human form to redeem the people from difficult times. We have been told how gods come down to the earth to interfere in man's affairs to help him to practise well and to shun evil. Thus, Vishnu appears under many guises. One of the most popular forms endeared, as a personal god, is that of the Lord Krishna, whose Divine Song, popularly known as the *Bhagvad Gita*, is still considered as one of the most sacred Hindu scriptures. The Gita is one of the rare holy books in Hinduism, which is used at innumerable circumstance to grace the occasion and make it pure and holy. The main role of Vishnu is that of the preserver of the universe. Thus, His intervening in human affairs has been quite frequent. His another form, popularly worshiped and adored by most Hindus has been in the guise of Rama, who has always been a source of inspiration possessing an ideal human conduct. Most Hindus, who are His devotees, often install a small statue of Rama in their personal small temple built at home to offer prayers.

Shakti also represents Lord Shiva's wife. She possesses extraordinary powers that have been bestowed upon Her by the three gods, Brahma, Vishnu and Mahesh (Shiva). Thus, She is also one of the most popular deities in Hinduism. There are stories that convey how She assists the gods and attempts most extraordinary feats that gods are unable to perform. Thus, Goddess Kali or Shakti has also inspired hundreds of Hindu devotees who constantly keep Her in mind and heart and continue worshiping her until they live. The best example in that respect is that of Sri Ramakrishna, who remained Her devotee until his last days and through his devotion, worship and insistence compelled Her to appear before him in human form to bless him.

The Western thinkers may easily get confused by a great number of gods and goddesses, who are popular in Hinduism. But if they are aware of the basic attitude of Hinduism that in substance all these divinities are identical and manifestation of the same divine reality, the confusion may be removed. The gods and goddesses, in their different forms, manifest the same divine reality that reflect different aspects of the infinite, who is Omnipresent, Omniscient, and— ultimately— incomprehensible, Brahman. Thus, the search of most Hindu minds ends with the understanding or knowing Brahman. It is also the stage of man's liberation or *moksha*.

So far most Hindu thinkers and theologians have constantly repeated and contented that man's search for the truth must end when *atman* unites Brahman. But there are some who have tried to discover it slightly differently. Neither denying nor approving the existence of Brahman and *atman*, they hold that *freedom* (Liberation) can still be attained provided man leads a life in accordance with a prescribed process. By following and practising the prescribed ways, the chain of death and re-birth would cease forever. It would be the highest stage of man's attainment where the search for truth would end. Thus, following some other paths too not prescribed by the *Vedas* in the ancient times can complete the quest for liberation and redeeming the self from the *samsara*. It is a fresh dimension in the development of Hinduism.

A New Awakening

A new wave of thought to liberate man from the chains of *samsara* has been projected by two great thinkers of the twentieth century. These men are Jiddu Krishnamurti and Acharya Rajneesh who by their uncanny approaches to human freedom have suggested new paths to proceed towards liberation. Both these metaphysicians gathered momentum during the middle of the twentieth century when the impact of Sri Yogananda's devotional methods had not completely ceased. Yogananda and Vivekananda were unparalleled contemporary god loving devotional *yogis,* who strongly projected their love and faith in the worship of the Highest. They unfurled the flag of Hinduism outside India and projected their *Vedantic* views before the world in a most convincing manner. In a *religious world congregation* Vivekananda held the Western intellectuals spellbound who had come to join the Religious Congress in Chicago. Though it was an already projected and advocated path by the Vedantins, these two great mendicants excelled in their approach in exhibiting simple ways to follow the religion. They showed extraordinary love and eagerness to project their feelings towards their faith and love for God. Their impact is still felt by the multitude Hindu population within and outside the country.

The two metaphysicians, Krishnamurti and Rajneesh, stated that man could attain the state of freedom and be free from the fetters of the world by following intellectual procedures. Although Gita has already prescribed that one, who desires to attain the Divine, can follow either devotional, *jnana* (knowledge) or *yoga margs.* In that respect both these intellectuals did not discover something absolutely new, as their approach to get freedom is also based on the *jnana marg*. Still their way is new in its own way. The newness lies in his or her procedures that so far have not been prescribed by anyone either in the sub-continent or in the Western world.

As a philosopher, Krishnamurti's position is quite unique. He developed neither any new philosophical canon, nor believed in any kind of practices, that would help man attain freedom gradually. He holds that man can reach the domain of freedom at once provided he keeps his mind free from every kind of thoughts. The thoughtless state of mind is the state of a meditative mind. It is also the state of a silent mind. In a most simple and convincing language, Krishnamurti reasserts the importance of the ancient precept 'know thyself' and advises humans to seek liberation by acquiring the right knowledge, which is the knowledge of one's own self.

Those who love philosophy and wish to acquaint themselves with Krishnamurti's views on human freedom would easily know that his approach towards human liberation is unique. During the question-answer sessions that he held in India, America and other advanced countries of the Western world, he analysed the human problems with great lucidity and depth and tried to convince the questioner with his excellent genius. The fathomless depth of his philosophical thinking and his reasoning capability are surely unparalleled. It is by his uncanny approaches towards human freedom that he has left indelible impact on most humans, especially the intellectual elite of the world. He has certainly added a new feather in the cap of Hinduism. Krishnamurti died after the age of ninety but he left many schools and missions that still run to propagate his ideas and philosophy.

Similarly, Acharya Rajneesh, during the later half of the twentieth century, showed an unusual way to attain freedom and spread the fragrance of his thoughts in the Eastern and the Western worlds. As a great logician, unbound by the old traditions of the Hindu religion, he projected new vistas of thought that represented the Truth, which not only made millions of humans understand it well, but convinced them too. Rajneesh initially hailed from the Jain religion, but he rejected most of the Jains' strict-procedures leading to attain liberation. He was one of the greatest philosophical analysts and orators India has ever produced in the past. When once I attended one of his lecture-sessions in India around thirty years back, I found him highly lucid in his explanations, which he often filled with real life examples. His unique style of arguing convinced the listeners instantly. Thus, like Krishnamurti he has a new approach towards the goal of freedom. Both Rajneesh and Jiddu Krishnamurti ardently condemn the ritualistic procedures to reach the threshold of freedom. They both try to convince that awareness towards 'one's own self' is the highest state of freedom, which provides ceaseless happiness too.

Thus, Hinduism has grown today like a banian tree that has many branches. Each of its branches looks very long and strong, and projects itself very distinctly. Though the developed dimension of each branch is immense, it is connected with the same stem. The impact of the ritualistic practices within the framework of the religion (Hinduism) has extremely been strong. It is so surprising that in spite of the fact that millions of inhabitants live in the sub-continent, but they practise almost similar kinds of customs and rituals even if their religious faiths are different. One can see this sort of unity among the people, especially during the naming ceremonies, marriages and demises. One can clearly see this kind of oneness during festivals and fairs that are organized time to time in the small hamlets, big towns and state capitals.

It is so unfortunate that some people, keeping in view their personal benefits, have lately infused some kind of religious bitterness among the people, but a great majority of the people still believes in living amicably, irrespective of their different faiths and religious practices. Thus, the beliefs and practices that originated a little before thousand years still have a strong hold on the masses in some way, in spite of multiple faiths they practise. That is the greatness of this august religion we call Hinduism.

The single-minded pursuit of the knowledge of Brahman, implying the attainment of *moksha*, has always provided this religion an enormous prestige. But the life of most Hindus is less directly concerned with seeking simply *moksha*. It is more attuned to conforming to the demands of *dharma* ('duty', 'order'), an important notion with a number of different meanings. It refers to an order with cosmic, moral, social and individual confines. *Dharma* has, in fact, established a kind of sacred order. It also directs what people ought to do and governs every aspect of human conduct, including everyday essential duties of life. Lord Krishna explained the form and the nature of duty of that kind a few thousand years before Christ. It has become a great source of inspiration to most Hindus throughout the world. The great Lord said,

> 'that man's right is to work only but he must not crave for its fruits. One should not reckon that one is the producer of the fruits of one's actions. Nor one should feel attached towards in action.' (Gita 2.47)

The Unparalleled Faith

All that has made Hinduism absolutely unparalleled. It may have different branches within its own dimensions, it may have variety in practising rituals, it may have a number of gods and goddesses to worship, but it teaches absolutely only one truth. The Creator of this world is only one—Brahman, Who since the beginning of this universe is begnningless and is present in all things even though they are transient. The same Brahman may be known by different names throughout the world by the people of different faiths, but the fact remains unchallenged. The idea of Brahman was revealed to the sages during the Vedic period just like the Ten Commandments were revealed to Moses before Christ.

The term Hindu perhaps originated from Iran. The Iranians, when gradually started knowing the people who lived on the other side of the river Indus, started calling them Hindus. Therefore, each one of us irrespective of practising any faith should feel proud to be a Hindustani. That conforms to what once Veer Savarkar had said about the inhabitants of India. Religion is purely a personal matter and, therefore, it must not come in the way of practising patriotism. Every individual who lives in Hindustan is a Hindu, irrespective of cultivating a different faith. It is agonizing that even educated people misunderstand the true meaning of religion. It is also painful that most people don't try to understand the meaning of duty, especially towards one's family, society and country. Everyone is free to cultivate one's own faith and worship as one pleases. Any sort of impediments in that respect is surely against the secular practices of a state that claims itself as a democratic country. Therefore, let no one misunderstand the meaning of religion and no kind of personal or religious practices should come in the way of our affinity towards the country. In fact, every faith has its own obligations. It must work to develop excellent conduct among individuals. It must provide right mindfulness to act in the right direction only. Any faith or religion, which unknowingly or mistakenly diverts individual's steps to an antisocial direction, is a wrong understanding of that faith. No faith or religion in the world directs any person to act against one's own brother. Hinduism has never taught to force its religious beliefs on others. It may have rigidity as far as the practices of rituals are concerned, but it has never forced itself upon others.

Lately, if there have been a very few unnoticed instances of that sort, that has happened on account of either retaliation or ignorance on the part of the convert. In that respect, Hinduism is certainly very liberal. I shall now enumerate the best in Hinduism in the following chapter.

Chapter Three

The Best in Hinduism

Notable Peculiarities

It is a fact of life that every thing, however good it may look, has the other side too. Hinduism is not an exception in that respect. It has some dark sides as well. Its dusky side is bounded mainly to some of its practices that led to revolt against it and consequently helped originating new religions within its own threshold. We have already referred to about its inadequacies in the previous chapter while describing its growth historically. Why the Aryans thought to offer sacrifices has also been briefly indicated earlier. The idea (to sacrifice) was perhaps originated as a result of man's fear of Nature. Man started invoking gods to pacifying them by offering sacrifices. But as time passed on there were repercussions against such practices. By the fifth century B.C., the great Buddha, Mahaveera and some other thinkers totally rejected the idea of sacrifice. They thought that 'sacrifice' could never be instrumental in developing amicable relationship between man and gods. Consequently, the belief that gods would intervene in man's affairs when required was also rejected.

There was another major impediment that proved detrimental to the practices of Hinduism. Too much involvement with the ritualistic practices gradually made it very stiff. It resulted in creating a new class in the society, which was free from any caste divisions until the Vedic- Brahminical period. During this period a class of Aryans, called the Brahmans, grew out of the multitude to help fulfill the ritualistic obligations of the people. The Brahmans gradually became so powerful that they started dictating terms to the people belonging to all walks of life. It happened mainly because they mastered the essential and appropriate verses to be chanted at the time of performing worship. In fact, they knew the secret of performing the art of sacrifice. Consequently, the Brahmans became a separate and stronger class in the society. It resulted in breaking up the entire society into a caste system. As the caste system developed, in the first few hundred years its adverse impact was very little, as it was created on the basis of the vocation of the people in the society. But gradually it started drifting into a different direction. With the rigidity and insolence on the part of the Brahmans, the labour class was gradually recognized as the untouchables. With the passage of time that class got branded as untouchables and suffered a lot in the hands of the upper classes. In spite of Indian Government's sincere efforts to remove the caste system from the society after the Independence, it still persists in the country. Gandhi, Nehru and almost all the leaders, who started the Indian Independence movement, tried very hard to abolish it, but its pangs are still felt by a great number of people. The lower classes especially the untouchables amongst them are great sufferers since long.

I would like to mention one more reason as an impediment against the proper growth of the religion. It is ignorance of the masses to understand correctly the meaning of religion. Since all duties in respect of conducting religious rituals were taken over by the Brahmans, the common man hired them to perform those rituals and to practise the traditional rites. Consequently, it led to further ignorance on the part of the general masses. They simply obeyed the Brahmans while performing the rituals without understanding any thing about them. It has still been going on for such a long time. As a result, the most ritualistically trained Brahmans, who feel equipped to discharge religious duties for others, have become very strong and hardheaded. As a result, they often start twisting the arms of their clients without caring for the financial and social background of an individual.

The worst of it can still be observed when one visits the

four *dhams* (most sacred places) to perform the traditional rituals, which are almost obligatory for each Hindu individual. A Hindu likes to visit these sacred places for his/her personal satisfaction or with a belief to trim the accumulated sins and to attain *moksha*. The priests, who mainly belong to the Brahman class, often identify a client from the throng and try to grab him/her for their personal benefits, mainly financial. I remember the incidence when I was travelling to Rameswaram in Tamil Nadu in India to pay my homage to Sri Rama. A religious agent, who happened to travel in my compartment, identified me as a potential client almost fifty miles before the main town. As soon as I alighted from the compartment, the agents and the priests surrounded me at the railway station. They persuaded me almost forcibly to stay at their desired place and tried to make me choose the priest of their choice to perform the rituals. I knew all that in advance as someone, who had travelled to that place earlier, had oriented me all about it. I did not permit them hold me for long. How can one, who calls himself a priest, sell nectar for the benefit of the others when he himself is inadequate and helpless in so many ways? Do the priests who are greed-infested have really any chance to be in the proximity of God? At Jagannath Puri at the Jagannath temple similar incidents happen when hundreds of devotees from all parts of the country visit the temple each day. How the priests try to extract money from their pockets is quite shameful and need to be stopped.

At this juncture I am reminded of an incidence that took place around forty years ago when I visited the famous Nathdwara temple at Nathdwara town near Udaipur in Rajasthan, India. The temple contains very comely statues of Sri Krishna and Radha. Hundreds of pilgrims, from dawn to dusk, visit there each day. Reaching the temple around 8 O'clock in the morning I tried to enter the main building. But a priest stopped me to enter as I was wearing a trouser and a shirt instead of a *dhoti* (a man's attire). I could not perform the *darshan* (to have a glimpse of the god) in want of a *dhoti* because the priest thought that it was impious to enter the temple in a western dress.

It was beyond my belief and satisfaction that how a temple priest, who would have not even taken bath or cleansed himself to perform his daily prayers, could stop me to enter the temple. How an ignorant like him can promise others to show God? At Rameswaram, another priest like the one I have referred to above, tempted me that he could get me God's real glimpse if I would give him certain amount of money. All the four sacred *dhams* and similar holy places are polluted by such imposter priests. They are wont to non-religious practices leading nowhere. Some of these adversaries still persist with the religions practices. As a results, many of those who are badly handled by the religious crooks at the holy places, feel disappointed and develop apathy towards their own beloved religion. These are the dark sides of the religion and its practices that perhaps initially did not exist with it. As time went by and human lust for money and material things accelerated, obsession of that nature started getting increased.

There are other kinds of imperfections too that were prevalent in the past as religious practices in Hinduism. Though many of them have now been dropped out as a result of public condemnation, some of them still persist. The truth is that no religious traditions, however old they may be, are totally free from such or similar kinds of shortcomings. Stories of child abuse and sex atrocities by the priests in the West were rampant throughout the world at the time when I was writing this chapter. Such ill-practices are widely condemned and stern actions are proposed against the offenders. Therefore, in spite of the fact that a number of shortcomings still exist with the Hinduism, an educated elite and a progressive person always looks at them with a critical eye. This kind of analytical view has resulted in bringing changes in religious practices in Hinduism. Because of people's strong desire to bring changes and to adhere to the best only, Hinduism has gradually evolved into a great religion. Many of its old traditions still survive. They have given it a great strength, which has really helped it survive for thousands of years. I shall, therefore, like to discuss now the best in Hinduism, which has been instrumental to keep it going, in spite of great impediments against it time to time.

The Peerless in the Religion

Hinduism has a number of unparalleled elements that make it a great religion of the world. These elements have helped it survive against various kinds of odds, especially forcible conversions of the people. These elements, which are the merits of this religion, are its strength and enumerate the best in it. It is because of such flourishing ideas as well as fruitful scientific practices that it has survived for thousands of years.

Liberalism

One of the best characteristics that has been helping Hinduism survive for so long is the element of liberalism. A Hindu is liberal in one's conduct to a great extent even though he/she is uneducated or not exposed to modern world. One of the best examples of a Hindu's liberality is his uncritical behaviour towards other religions. He would hardly condemn his neighbour on account of his/her practising a different religion even if he was emotionally unhappy with the neighbour's conservative conduct. I have seen how a Hindu individual would gladly visit a church or a *durgah* (a Muslim religious place) at the festive occasions and meet the people there with open arms with the same emotional intensity with which he likes to meet his own religious mates. But any person of the other religious faith would hardly visit a Hindu temple for the unfounded fear of becoming sinful. A Hindu is often condemned for idol worshipping. But is it not true that people belonging to the major religions of the world worship idol or stone in one form or the other. I am not stating it just to condemn the practices of other religions, but I simply wish to highlight that most great religions of the world have some kind of commonness with each other? That commonness can easily be identified provided the people of other religious faiths don't look at others' traditions with a prejudiced eye. Blind love and attachment for our own religious practices may often lead us to condemn the other's precious practices.

Hinduism approves both kinds of practices— one with the

idol worshipping and the other without it. One with the idol is known as the *sakar* (with the object) way of worship and the other without it is known as *nirakar* (without object) worship. Sri Ramakrishna's is the best example in that respect. He initially started his *puja* (worship) invoking the *sakar*. After some time when he met his *guru*, Totapuri, he became a *nirakar* devotee. The idol is simply the medium to concentrate upon an object (God), which is so difficult to conceive or meditate. Even if it is an idol worshipping on the part of a Hindu, how others have the privilege to attack him/her on that account. Is it not disgusting and a matter of great dismay that those who worship God through idols condemn others for the same reason?

There are other aspects of liberalism in Hinduism that need to be enumerated. I am not talking of the variety in religion at this point when I express that a Hindu enjoys a unique kind of freedom in religion. It is that in a Hindu family the father may be a devotee of Krishna, the mother may worship Rama while the son or the daughter may be a devotee of Shakti (Goddess Kali) or Ganesha. Not only that, they have separate timings for their worshipping, they also install different idols in the small temple of the house to worship the deity they like most. It is not normally seen with the devotees of the other religions. Well, by stating so I am not enumerating shortcomings of any other religion, but I am simply reflecting how much a Hindu devotee enjoys freedom while worshipping or praying. It is also quite unique that on account of different emphasis on different gods on the part of the members of a family, no ill-will generates among them. How many examples of that nature one can really quote from the other religions of the world I really know not, but if some examples are available they are not very many.

Variety, not Stagnation

With the kind of liberality and freedom stated above, Hinduism enjoys a unique position and privilege in the entire world. Not only it is a religion that can bring contentment and satisfaction to its followers, it is a religion of great variety that helps meeting every one's requirement. Here, by requirement I don't mean fulfilment of one's physical needs. I simply mean satisfaction of the spiritual requirement. I have already stated that in the variety there lies unity that binds all into one. But each individual has his own psychological needs and in line with that he/she tries to discover his/ her own religious practices. Thus, different gods are great source of satisfaction to different individuals.

Therefore, each god is highly honoured and becomes focus of attention of unlike individuals. Each god has his own specialty, his/her own power to bestow on his/her devotees. If one wants to excel in learning, one needs to worship Saraswati, the goddess of learning. If one desires to amass wealth, one can go for worshipping Laxmi, the goddess of wealth. Like that each god has some thing to give to every one. Examples of that kind would easily be found in the Indian villages where people are content by worshipping *Behron* or other lesser gods. But every Hindu understands that there lies an underlying unity behind each of these gods and goddesses. That unity is seen in the form of Brahman or Vishnu, who is Omnipotent, and the Creator of the entire universe. Thus, the idea of variety, which was initiated from the very beginning when man started worshipping the elements of nature, is still contained in the religion. It not only provides a kind of personal satisfaction, it also stops stagnation as no one is bound to go for only one kind of god.

Let us not forget that it is man's nature to seek variety. For if he does not do so he could stagnates. It is simply not for the sake of variety only that one seeks different gods, but it is also that one wants to get some more in one field than the other. So he/she seeks different gods and goddesses. Is it not surprising as well as a testimony to my idea of 'one's desire in seeking this kind of variety', that only different gods and goddesses are worshipped at the occasion of festivals in many provinces in India? For example, in Bengal it is the goddess Kali who is worshipped during the Dipawali (festival of lights) days; it is Ganesha who is worshipped in Maharashrta, and it is Jagannath (Sri Krishna) who is worshipped in Gujrat and Orrisa. Sri Rama, though worshipped throughout the country, is especially honoured in Utter Pradesh, Tamil Nadu, Madhya Pradesh and Rajasthan. While Durga, another name of Shakti, is worshipped in Rajasthan, Bengal and many other provinces, as she is the fountain of power that one requires throughout one's life. It is most important and a point to be noted that in worshipping different gods and goddesses a Hindu never gets frustrated by the other worshiper. He would never fight or condemn a Ganesh *upasak* (devotee) for he himself worships Laxmi, the goddess of wealth. We have plenty of examples from other religions where apparently there is hardly any bifurcation as far as worshipping is concerned yet a little departure from the usual norm has brought massacres of thousands of innocent people. There lies the strength of Hinduism that in spite of the variety, there is hardly any kind of frustration or enigma among its people. People are free to worship different gods and goddesses in the same house or in a hamlet, which is inhabited by a very thin population.

The Implicit -Kindness

There is nothing very specific in reflecting upon the element of kindness in Hinduism in comparison to the major religions of the world, which contain this kind of gracious element. Yet it is necessary to reflect upon it while enumerating its strong points. One of the best examples of that kind can be taken from the life of the ancient great Indian king Ashoka, who after the Kalinga war relinquished fighting, as he could not stand the sight of the massacre of hundred thousand people. It is stated that right after that war he accepted Buddhism and sent his daughter and son as ambassadors to the neighbouring countries to spread the teachings of Buddha. It is obvious that the sight of that great massacre must have ignited a feeling of kindness in the heart of Ashoka that he felt impelled to send emissaries to other countries with peaceful tidings. No country of the world has such a record if it ever tried to spread its religion. Almost all the great religions of the world have been extended either at the point of sword or through strong persuasion implied with some kind of fear. At times, instead of fear, different kinds of temptations have also been offered to spread religion. Often, great force and fear of death have brought conversions. When the invaders from the north in the 11th century A.D. attacked India, it is said that the Chandnichowk, one of the main markets of Delhi, was flooded with human blood, as the number of the people killed by the invaders was extremely phenomenal.

It would be untrue to say that other religions don't possess the element of kindness with them, but kindness is certainly imbedded in Hinduism from the very beginning. Parents from early childhood teach their children to be kind to others. Kindness to animals and even to insects is emphasized to each individual from the early childhood by the elders and through legends. If there are few bad examples to be quoted against it, they are certainly bad and uncommon instances. Let me quote a few incidents, which occurred during Hindu-Muslim riots in India, when act of kindness on the part of Hindu individuals saved the lives of the Muslims at the cost of their own lives. At many occasions during riots when some wild people came running in the middle of the night to kill the only Muslim family living in the Hindu populated areas, often a Hindu family gave shelter to that family and extended complete shelter and security to it. It has often happened that a Hindu has displayed kindness of that nature and saved the families of the people belonging to the other religion. But that kind of example is not frequently seen with the people of other religions. It is perhaps because the element of kindness in Hinduism has been propagated from the very start. Hatred has never been the dimension of Hindu religion any time even though some headstrong people would have displayed it sometimes.

The religions, which originated from Hinduism, have always displayed the element of love and kindness too. Buddhism and Jainism, which are the offshoots of Hinduism, have always appreciated and displayed the importance of kindness. We all know how Gautama (later on Buddha) refused to hand over the wounded pigeon to his cousin who had shot at it. When Gautama took out the arrow from its body and started tending it, the cousin demanded the pigeon for he had shot at him. Gautama refusing to give it to him said, 'one who saves a life has more right on it than the one who tries to kill it.' *'Bahujan hitaya and bahujan sukhaya'* is a very popular thought of a Hindu that he often chants during prayers or even during ordinary conversation. It simply means that one should act for 'the benefit and happiness of others' only. No one can learn kindness unless people practise it in the family. It is a point to be noted that Hindu scriptures teach kindness even towards ants and other small insects. Therefore, when a Hindu walks he would often try not to trample any insects.

Hinduism, All Accommodating

It is a matter of great satisfaction that Hinduism, though it has certain inadequacies, has always acted like an elder brother to other religions, especially those, which have originated on account of revolt against it. Except that there are casual examples of the nature where some so-called pundits have criticized other offshoots of Hinduism, most Hindus are humble and accommodating to the other religions. For example, Sikhism, Jainism or Buddhism, which grew as a result of revolting against Hinduism, have hardly been rejected or criticized by it. On the contrary, most Hindus have accepted the founders of these religions as *avtars* (incarnation) of gods. Not only Buddha but Mahaveera and Guru Nanak as well have since been accepted as incarnations of god or great religious leaders. It has been the greatness of Hinduism that the religions, which condemned it and which were highly critical against it, were hardly rejected by it.

The basic truth is that the ideas that were developed by the other religions after revolting against certain practices of Hinduism were simply taken from Hinduism. For example, it was through rejecting the practice of 'sacrifice' in Hinduism that Buddha and Mahaveera laid the foundation of their own religious practices. Besides, Mahaveera and Buddha also rejected the thought that 'gods intervene in human affairs and come down to the earth to help them.' Instead of gods helping the individual to keep a straight line, both Buddha and Mahaveera suggested that man himself should lead a life that would help him practising right conduct. Buddha suggested 'eight-fold-path to attain *nirvana*' or salvation. Mahaveera also recommended similar code of conduct to practise for the attainment of *nirvana*. Thus, if certain aspects of Hinduism were rejected by its offshoots, those very aspects became the source of inspiration for them. In this manner Hinduism helped its own byproducts to thrive in future. No other religion would have directly or indirectly helped its rival religion to flourish at all.

Visiting the Dhams

It is so amazing that thousands of years ahead, Hinduism approved visiting the four *dhams* as a part of its religious practices. Perhaps more than the fulfilment of religious commitment, the main idea behind those visits was to know and feel about the different kinds of people who live in different parts of India. There is no better way to understand the people and comprehend their religious practices than to observe and live in their proximity. The great ancient sages who mostly loved to live in the forests visualized that unity of this heterogeneous country could only be maintained if people knew each other thoroughly. Thus, the practice to visit the religious places (*dhams*) came into vogue among the people. Besides, installation of each cherished Hindu deity was made in four different and distant directions so that each Hindu should try to visit those places on account of religious obligations. It was never compulsory for a Hindu individual to visit these sacred places in his/her lifetime, but gradually it became almost obligatory for him/her to visit these holy places. But one who can visit and one who is not able to visit the holy places is equally good as far as religious practices are related. There is, in fact, more stress on the cultivation of good human conduct within the framework of religion than to be involved with the practices of that kind so strictly. It is certainly unlike the other religions where evidently such practices are insisted and made compulsory. It is another great example of liberalism in Hinduism.

There is another utility implicit in visiting the four *dhams*, besides religious obligation. The *dhams* are situated in four different provinces of the country. These regions are infused with such a variety of natural loveliness that you cannot miss the extraordinary comeliness of the nature when you go to visit them. Take for example, when we go to Badrinath in the extreme north, we find ourselves amid total serenity. The mountains, emerging suddenly behind the Badrinath temple, often covered with snow, provide a stunning scene, which is not only extraordinary, but goes on humming in one's mind forever. What a scene, so comely and impressive! Who would go to visit these places to enjoy the beauty of nature when our daily demands never let us have a chance to come out from the busy routine of life? It will really be unfortunate to miss these places in our lives only because we don't possess any desire to do so.

Similarly, when we travel to Dwarka, Jagannathpuri or Rameswaram, we observe vast seas spreading beyond our sight. What a fascinating sight it is! It suddenly captivates one's heart and brings in it a renewed sense of extreme adoration for these religious places endowed with wonderful natural bounty. In this manner, the visits to these holy places is not limited to pay homage to the gods but also to feel and live with the nature. Normally, it is not possible to live by the nature or to enjoy its comely presence. People are so busy with their personal commitments that they hardly get a chance to peep out of that. Therefore, visiting the holy places is a blessing in disguise. Once when I visited Kannyakumari, the last tip of the Indian subcontinent near Sri Lanka, I observed how waters of the three seas meet at a point right at the end of the last tip. It was evening and the full moon had started tracing its route in the sky. Sitting at an empty boat, I observed that something extremely fascinating was happening at the meeting point of the seas. Is it not nature's astonishing feat to make the three seas meet at a point and create a heavenly sight for the onlookers? Thus, amazing enjoyment and pleasure is implied when we visit the holy places. Besides providing a sense of obligatory fulfilment, these visits also impart celestial enjoyment in the company of the nature. Who would have thought so in advance that visiting the holy places would be so much rewarding! The ancient sages had such an insight that they could visualize all that in advance and, therefore, added it within the framework of religion. Hinduism, therefore, is a very rich religion in that sense.

Endless Moral Contact

The epics, the *Ramayana* and the *Mahabharata,* containing the accounts of the exploits of gods in human form, living on earth and fighting for the cause of human beings, have always influenced the moral life of the Hindu individual. It is a permanent belief of a Hindu that gods incarnate on the earth to fight against the evil and for the establishment of good. These Epics have served throughout Hindu history assuring the Hindu that gods act on behalf of humans. The epics have been the primary sources along with the later *Puranas* for the inculcation of moral ideals that have continuously been influencing individual's conduct, irrespective of his/her position in the society. It is a matter of great rejoicing and self-esteem that at the time of a Hindu marriage, or someone's demise in the family or even at the child's birth, it is the name of Rama, which is remembered and chanted with great respect. Most Hindus, while saluting one another when they meet first during the day, chant Ram's name. Besides Rama, Sri Krishna, god's another *avtara,* has equally influenced the Hindu way of life. The *Bhagvad Gita* has always been considered as a basic holy treatise (discource), that a Hindu respects dearer than his life. Consequently, the impact of these epics has not only been colossal but continuous also. There is no Hindu family where *Ramayana* is not read and studied by the young and the elders. Almost all Hindus chant some slokas (verses) from the *Bhagvad Gita* or utter Rama's name when they are about to go for the final slumber (demise). This sort of impact has created an endless moral environment, which reminds each Hindu man or woman to shun acting immorally.

Duty for Duty's Sake

There are other important things that need to be mentioned at this juncture. The ancient Aryans always put a lot of thought when they included something with the religious practices. For example, at someone's demise in the family, his/her bones after cremation are mostly taken to Haridwar to be immersed in the river Ganga because it is considered sacred. It, therefore, provides an opportunity for a change of place and environment for the person who carries the bones to the holy place. Mostly, it is an obligation on the part of the eldest son of the demised to perform the last rituals. Thus, it not only gives him a break from the doleful environment of the family, it also provides him an opportunity to reflect about the ways of the world at the holy place. While immersing the bones into the sacred river, at times he might leap into serious thoughts, and be reminded that every thing in this world is transitory. Therefore, he must involve himself in good acts and should not evade his duties towards others without thinking of any returns. It is one of the noblest thoughts suggested by the seers to keep in mind by the followers of the Hinduism. Thus, the notion 'duty for duty's sake' is extremely popular among the Hindus and is literally chanted in almost every Hindu family when one does not get results/rewards of his actions. The *Bhagvad Gita* has very aptly reminds the man about it when Sri Krishna admonishes Arjuna to fulfill his duty without any desire of the fruits. It says,

कर्मण्येवाधिकारस्ते मा फलेषु कदाचन ।
मा कर्मफलहेतुर्भूर्मा ते सङ्गोऽस्त्वकर्मणि ॥४७॥

Thy right is to work only; but never to the fruits thereof.
Be thou not the producer of the fruits of (thy) actions;
Neither let thy attachment be towards inaction. (2.47)*

If we skip through the holy pages of any religious book of the major religions of the world, such a notion towards one's duty would hardly be seen. The *Bhagvad Gita* has thus influenced a common man's life in many ways and in different aspects. Besides the concept of duty, it also provides a clear view about the world. The world is simply transitory. It is on account of our ignorance that we start reckoning the world in terms of kingship, attachment and various sorts of emotional involvement. Thus, the *Gita* provides a right direction to each individual to follow so that he/she can attain the final goal in life. The best part of that kind of advice is the choice of persuasion of any of the various paths that would lead one to salvation or *moksha*. Most major religions of the world suggest only one procedure to know God. It is deep devotion only. There lies the greatness of Hinduism, which suggests at least three ways to attain *moksha* or reach the domain of Brahman. Let us briefly reflect upon them once again to emphasize that though the procedures of each path are different, but each one of them ultimately leads to the same direction. It is the direction leading towards the God's realm only. Each procedure, though varied, has the same effect on one's soul if one follows it dogmatically.

Multiple Paths for Emancipation

I have already briefly discussed in the previous chapter the various ways of liberation suggested in Hinduism. In fact, it is one of the most creditable aspects of Hinduism that it is highly liberal even about the procedures of attaining *moksha*. It provides almost three clear ways to reach God's realm. The *Bhagvad Gita* supports this view and approves of the three ways to attain salvation. These three ways are, the *path of the knowledge*, the *way of action,* and *the way of devotion* which has been followed by many devotees and is highly popular in the East and the West as well.

One of the most popular and intellectual schools of Indian philosophy, Vedanta, which is based on the *Upanishads*, emphasizes that the *way of knowledge* is the best way to reach the final goal of life. Brahman is non-personal and is entirely free from any formal description. To concentrate on something, which has no form or qualities, is surely not an easy destination to reach. But the Vedantins approve of daily meditation and suggest different kinds of spiritual exercises to reach Brahman. The only final goal, according to Samkara, is meeting Brahman.

In fact, the *atman* is the part of Brahman and when it is united with Brahman, it becomes one with it and attains liberation. The *atman* is not able to reach Brahman on account of ignorance, on account of taking the world as real. Only the wise men know how to be free from the illusory (Maya) world and remain detached from it. Thus, it is the way of knowledge, which transports one from illusion and elevates him/her to the domain of Brahman.

Samkara first tried to prove the existence of the self. Thus, he upheld the Upanishadic ideology that an entity (*atman*) within the human being is related in some way with Brahman. Then he held that the *atman* is independent of human body. It is also independent of the mental or psychic aspects of the human being. The fundamental error an individual makes is to identify the self with the body or the mind. Thus, false understanding of something, which is not there, leads to ignorance. Therefore, the primary cause of this ignorance is the confusion of the observed with the Ultimate Reality. It is because of ignorance that rebirth take place. The pains in life and conceiving the world as real are the result of ignorance. Hence, true knowledge of *samsara* or the world is essential to attain *moksha*. Thus, the *way of knowledge* is of great importance, according to the Vedantins.

Besides Samkara, the most modern philosophers who have re-stressed the importance of this approach are Jiddu Krishnamurti and Acharya Rajneesh who emphasize the importance of *the way of knowledge* to attain liberation. Rajneesh's procedure is purely intellectual. He is contended with analytical ways to reach the Truth. While Krishnamurti, though intellectual, has quite a different approach to attain freedom. He suggests that it is on account of various impediments that a human is not able to attain freedom. These impediments are conditioning and inadequate knowledge of the self about itself. It is because of the inadequacy of the clear knowledge created because of conditioning that one is not able to attain freedom. Krishnamurti asserts that through self-knowledge and awareness one can easily reach the final goal of life, which is nothing other than freedom. It is not the political freedom that he speaks of but simply the freedom of the mind. Thus, he acknowledges that the path of knowledge is a sure way to attain freedom.

The *way of action* or deed (*karma*) is another important approach to seek God. Through this way an individual, by performing his religious kind of sacrifices and fulfilling the social responsibilities of his station in life, completes his *dharma*. In fact, to a large extent it is a continuation of the Vedic-Brahmanic tradition, which is still fulfilled at different occasions in one's life, especially when the child is born in the family, at the time of a marriage and when someone dies. Certain traditions, which were incorporated as a part of individual's social duty during Vedic-Brahmanic period, are still quite popular though they may not be fulfilled in an extensive manner. Although much has been changed and minimized as far as the old rituals and traditions are concerned, a Hindu feels dissatisfied and less contended unless he/she discharges the traditional obligations in his family. When he/she has finally performed all the social duties, a great satisfaction ensues within him/her, which provides total contentment and peace. It is also a state of freedom.

I remember a short meaningful tale at this juncture relating to the issue of discharging one's social obligations completely. Someone desirous of getting *jnana* (right knowledge), left his home, abandoned his children and wife, and reached a hermit's abode to attain the right knowledge so that he could attain salvation. When a few months passed at the hermitage, the *guru* observed the seeker closely. He found that the seeker seemed to be lost in something else and was not praying with full attention as advised. On inquiry, the man replied the hermit that he often remembered his wife and children whom he had left without any help. Therefore, he was not able to concentrate thoroughly. The hermit then advised him to go back home and take care of his family before he thought to come to his hermitage. The man left as advised and found that the sage was right. Sri Krishna suggested the same path to Arjuna during the Mahabharata when he felt confused and bewildered.

Lastly, the *way of devotion*, which involves our love and

ardent worship to a personal God. It was supported by the theological system of Vedantic thinkers like Ramanujam and Madhavacharya. Ramanujam, during the eleventh century, emphasized the reality of the world, the individual self and the Brahman. Ramanujam holds that Brahman is primary and both the world and the individual selves of men depended upon Brahman. The self comes from Brahman, but it remains detached, though a dependent unit. Ramanujam holds that *moksha* can be obtained by the knowledge of Brahman, which comes through meditation and devotion and necessary addition of the divine grace of the Brahman. In fact, Brahman responds to the deep devotion of the self and bestows on it its grace by endowing on it all its qualities. Thus, he holds that the self can be released from the *samsara* and be united with Brahman forever.

Similarly, Madhavacharya, in the thirteenth century, held that Brahman was eternal. He also believed in the permanence of the selves and the *samsara* but they were not equal to Brahman. They are dependent upon it. Madhava holds that Vishnu and Brahman are the same, therefore, devotion to Krishna as an *avtara* of Vishnu is devotion to Brahman. In this manner, it is the Vedanta that laid the foundation of Hindu religious thought and devotion. Madhava holds that *moksha* is possible from *samsaric* (worldly) limitations through devotion and the chain of rebirth can be stopped when the soul is in perfect relationship with Brahman. It is the most blissful relationship with the Divine. The *bhakti* (devotion) expression of Hinduism primarily concentrates on the worship of some aspect of the great gods, Vishnu or Shiva, and goddesses like Shakti or Kali. The literary basis of the *bhakti* is the Puranic literature and the epics, mainly the *Bhagvad Gita*. The *Puranas* have greatly served as the means of transporting the popular understanding of gods and their activities in relationship to man. Such ideas have been made known to the vast majority of the Hindus in India and abroad by means of dance and drama. Thus, the path of devotion has been held as one of the lucid paths to attain the Divine.

There are innumerable examples of that kind during the

past hundreds and thousands of years when the ardent devotees of God have claimed their union with Him and have ventured to reach His abode by their steady love and attachment towards Him. Christ, Joan of Arc, Mohammed, Tulsidas, Meera, Ramakrishna, Yogananda, Vivekananda, and many more have been God's committed devotees who claimed to have communion with Him or even talked to Him. In fact, the way of devotion is the only path that is mostly popular in the West. But Hinduism has different approaches to lead us to find the way to God's abode. Besides the above three, there is one more way to get liberation. It is through Patanjali's *Yoga*, which is becoming extremely popular in the West too. Though *Yoga* can be categorized under the *karma marg* (way of action), it has great contribution and hope as far as man's liberation is concerned.

The teaching of great significance for Hinduism that became clearly evident in the post-Upanishadic period is that of *Yoga*. The simple meaning of *Yoga* is 'yoke' or 'discipline'. It is reported that *Yoga* definitely is of ancient origin. It began to appear as a distinct practice to control mind and body during the ancient times when the *gurus* ran their ashrams for the education of their pupils mostly in the forests. Three factors were considered important in *Yoga*. (i) The idea of gaining power by meditation and self-denial that was at the heart of its teaching; (ii) Understanding the Upanishadic distinction between essential self and material self; and (iii) Continuous and increasing stress upon the ability of the ultimate self to control the body. These three aspects of *Yoga* made it widely accepted in the Indian religion. In fact, at the heart of *Yoga* is the assurance that *moksha* requires the individual to be detached from the *samsaric* (world) attachments. It is quite apparent that first step to get the release from the *samsaric* bonds is to control the body's actions by the basic self. For such a discipline, it is imperative to have a well-experienced *guru* who would help not only in practising *Yoga* techniques, but also direct to the way leading to *moksha*. Considering its good effects on the body and mind of an individual practitioner, *Yoga* became popular with every Indian religion. It has been a long-standing Indian belief that the spirit (soul) is absolutely different from the physical body. Therefore, by proper disciple one can obtain *moksha*.

Rich Philosophical Treasure

It is a matter of great self-esteem and satisfaction that there are at least six Indian schools of philosophy, which grew out of the basic human desire and need to get salvation from the transient world and to understand the nature of Reality. Some of these schools developed side by side as a matter of reaction or fulfilment towards the other. But some grew as the sage learnt how to transcend the ordinary level of perception. In the beginning and for hundreds of years these notions and traditions were handed over down to the generations orally. Once when the *sutras* and ideas were put on the paper (paper of any quality, or even a dried leaf), in a short span of time great literature of philosophical notions developed.

The *Vedas* are said to have been revealed at a time we exactly don't know, but there is a rough idea of time of certain schools of philosophy, which grew as a reaction against the Vedic traditions. Except the *Vedas*, every school of philosophy was created by a *rishi* (a hermit of great wisdom), who reflected in a unique way to know about the nature of Reality or Truth, and tried to discover how man could attain *moksha* ultimately. There lies the main difference between the Western and the Eastern philosophical way of thinking. The West is more inclined to search about the Truth and the realities that exist within the span of a human life or in the universe. What is more valuable for man in this world and what can bring him greater success and happiness, are the dearest premises they are interested in. In that sense the Western philosophers are comparatively more pragmatic. The themes that they often ponder over are happiness, tranquillity, dismay, disappointment, failure and success in human lives.

The Eastern thinkers are also practical as regards the practices to reach God's realm are concerned. Their way of thinking is often, therefore, branded as mythical, for God's realm is unknown and can be attained without external verification. These philosophers often don't run after the physical pleasures as they reckon them the sources of pain and agony in this world. Any one who seeks such pleasures is an ignorant individual who has lost the right path in life. The ultimate goal of the Eastern philosopher is the unity of the spirit with the Brahman, the Ultimate Truth. Thus, the East is more inclined to discover the Truth in relation to man's release from this transient world and to get freedom from the ailments of life. In that sense, the Eastern approach, though it may be considered mystic by the Western thinkers, is certainly more pragmatic in nature. How far the pleasures of life go with man? It is certainly an important issue to be understood by each individual at an early stage of life. If he would not do so, he may be bewildered during rest of his life. The great Indian ancient sages through their analytical and metaphysical reflections had discovered that the way of life is not the pursuit of sensuous pleasures, but to seek a greater truth about it. That truth was to shun the sensuous kind of life and follow a spiritual way to attain tranquillity and endless bliss. That is why they advocated leading a different kind of life.

During the *Sutra* period, the Indian philosophical traditions associated themselves with the *Vedas* and began to systematize their beliefs. Consequently, a great consciousness grew towards special activities of different traditions. The early centuries of the first millennium A.D. observed a synthesis of philosophical and theological ideas into various schools of philosophy. It laid the foundation of the six distinct Indian schools of philosophy that has already been stated a little while ago. Besides certain uncommon practices among them, each of the schools was acknowledged as being equally valid to help attaining *moksha*. These schools are divided into two distinct categories—the *astika* and the *nastika*. The Buddhism and the Jainism are the *nastika* schools of philosophy, which don't accept the primacy of Brahman. The rest of the schools of Indian philosophy recognize in one way or the other the existence of Brahman as the Ultimate Reality, and hold that it is the source of all evolution in the universe. These orthodox schools can be paired together into three groups, which are: *Nyaya* and *Vaisesika*, *Samkhya* and *Yoga*, and *Mimamsa* and *Vedanta*. Individually, these schools are concerned with various philosophical aspects such as epistemology (knowledge), logic, physics, how the matter was evolved, aesthetics etc. But all these schools have their separate identity and influence on the Indian way of life. Each school, besides the Vedanta, which has a greater acceptability and identification, has in its own way contributed towards the belief in the existence of Brahman. Thus, all are held to be a *darshan*, which means 'a looking at' the truth.

Although the Buddha and mainly the Jain systems of thought are quite popular within the Indian sub-continent, it is Vedanta that has served predominantly as the expression of Hindu religion. We have already discussed briefly within Vedanta the different schools of thought that have occupied the Hindu thought process for good. Thus, Indian schools of philosophy have always dominated the Hindu mind and have influenced their life-pattern since the dawn of the Vedantic knowledge. The impact of the various sorts of religious ideologies has been so immense that neither communism nor materialism has ever been able to claim a firm footing on the simple, less-affluent Hindu way of life. A Hindu is satisfied with less materialistic possessions for his/her way of life, is dominated with a belief that there is yet another world besides the existing one, which is permanent and lasting. Merely this kind of notion has governed the Indian way of thinking since the ancient times, and has directed it into a way, which apparently and deeply seems to be more satisfying and blissful as well. There lies the richness of the Indian philosophical traditions.

Chapter Four

Hinduism Redefined

We have so far discussed Hinduism historically, enumerated its beliefs and identified the best that still exists in the religion. But some thing imperative still needs to be discussed. It is the need to discuss the issues that are related to a Hindu's conduct or his/her responsibilities towards the people and society. In spite of the fact that the epics and the *Puranas* still have their stronghold on the common man's way of thinking, many Hindu individuals feel free to act in their own way and lead a life which is neither much beneficial to them nor to the community. That means departure from a prescribed path has a very little meaning for them. Yet they are still Hindus because the society is very liberal. No one cares much for those who drift away from the traditional ways. When I mention 'traditional way(s)', I don't mean an absolute observance of the ritualistic procedures in vogue for long. I simply mean those practices that are followed either at the time of the child's naming ceremony, initiation at the occasion of the sacred thread ceremony, or marriage ceremony, etc.

In fact, I met and interviewed people informally in India and abroad during the past two years and tried to find out 'what minimum they expect a Hindu practitioner to do to stay firmly with his/her fold' I would like to sum up this chapter with what people have strongly expressed in that respect and what minimum practices they expect a Hindu must do if Hinduism has to survive and flourish in future. In light of this, I would like to focus first on the issues that have become impediments to the growth of Hinduism. After that I would discuss 'what minimum a Hindu individual is expected to do to perpetuate and enrich the age-old religion.' Along with it, I would also redefine the beliefs that are the basis of the religion and are its strongholds for a couple of thousand centuries.

Impediments against Hinduism

There are various issues that are obviously impediments to the growth of Hinduism. Some of these issues have been discussed hereunder to bring home to the reader how these obstacles barricade the easy growth of Hinduism.

Apathy for Rituals

It is a fact of life that the practices that are abandoned die out gradually. If we look at the Hindu practices that were usually popular in the past, we find that many of them have either been polluted or even dropped out. Say for example, when a child would go to school for the first time in life, a proper ceremony used to be held by almost all the Hindu families in the past. Again, most Hindu families would have a small *tulsi* plant within the compound of their houses. All ladies would worship it regularly, especially at dawn and twilight. There is some kind of utility (mainly hygienic) of the plant within the house. Scientific investigations have proved it too that the plant does not permit to grow certain kinds of insects in the house. Therefore, our ancestors made it a ritualistic necessity to keep a small *tulsi* plant in the house and worship it regularly. It is hardly practised these days.

One may say what is the use of those kinds of practices and ceremonies in a rapidly growing scientific age? Well, practices are useful, as most of them are cultivated for the growth of the race and the community. Ceremonies are the strong social threads within a culture that keep the community stay together. Very often it may look that they don't have any separate utility or benefit but their regular practice provides some sort of happiness the individual, who performs them regularly. Involving oneself willingly with a ceremony brings a vivid understanding in an individual that he/she belongs to a particular community or religion. Therefore, rituals and ceremonies are of great utility.

There is another kind of benefit by a truthful observance of a ceremony. It often brings an untold joy to people who participate in it. For example, during a marriage ceremony, besides a Hindu priest, who performs the marriage rituals, there are a number of other relatives and people who participate in the ceremony in their own way. Ladies have a major share at such occasions. They make the opportunity absolutely comely by their music and dance. Local dances and songs sung at different occasions during a marriage make everything look absolutely fascinating. Marriages, that are held in a hurry on account of any reason(s) what so ever, provide much less happiness and pleasure to both the parties. People do like to indulge in ceremonies and perform the rituals for socialization as well as for their personal satisfaction and enjoyment. Therefore, it would not be true to say that the ceremonies have no place in today's busy schedule of life. However busy one may be, one would like to involve with certain activities that are in vogue for such a long time. It would not be quite beneficial to curtail the customs or practices that have been dearly held by the community in the past. There lies the strength of the community and the society too when such activities are continued with a desire to perpetuate them.

New Traditions and Changing Beliefs

There has been a strange kind of pressure on account of 'lack of time' on the minds of most of the young people of every community in India in the modern age. The young men, belonging to the Hindu community, are perhaps affected most on that account. Every thing that they like to do they measure not with its utility criterion but with the availability of time at their disposal. With the pretext of 'lack of time', they often like to evade performing any kind of old customs. Although the main reason to rebel against performing a ritual or a tradition is a dislike towards it for it belongs to the old stock, most of the time they postpone the execution of a ritual or a tradition only because they fear that they don't have time. Consequently, new practices are gradually taking place in place of the older ones. There is nothing wrong to introduce new practices at the time of certain occasions or ceremonies, but they must be suitable as well as enjoyable to all.

Take for example the practice of *women folk going with the marriage parties* along with men folk. In India, often marriages take place at a different destination than the bridegrooms hometowns. It is because of that reason that the bridegroom, his father, relatives and friends need to go to the bride's hometown to perform the marriage ceremony. A few years back, say during nineteen seventies, the marriage parties were comprised with malefolk only. But it is a recent development that ladies also join the marriage parties. Perhaps, this sort of custom has also come in practice on account of better hotel and other facilities for women. There is nothing wrong in women's joining a marriage party. But in view of different kinds of problems that practice can be abandoned. One of such problems is the excessive use of hard drinks on the part of a few men who are with the marriage party. One can imagine the situation when some men under the spell of drinks may misbehave with the women. It can cause a chain of problems that include fighting, abusing each other and denouncing people for no reason.

It is just a hypothetical situation that I have indicated here, but in reality many kinds of difficulties may suddenly be created for the father of the bridegroom who is responsible to look after all the guests who join the marriage party at his request. Just imagine the scene of a good marriage ceremony performed in a totally sacred environment. When two priests regularly chant Sanskrit *slokas* (verses) and all the guests sitting nearby the *mandap* (a small decorated tent to be used to perform the marriage ceremony) watch the bride and the bridegroom sit cross-legged in front of fire performing the rituals as directed by the priests. What a celestial scene! It simply fills the guests and the relatives with mirth and untold joy. In such a congenial environment, there is always a good talk between the relatives of both the sides. Every one seems to be taking care of each other. The marriage takes place amid sweet music and sweet talks instead of abuses, drunkenness and fighting. Therefore, if women accompany a marriage-party, it is imperative that men-folk must take care of them properly and drunkenness should not occur when the marriage party is staying as a guest of the bride's father.

Something else has been added at the occasion of marriages in the name of modernism. It is *dancing of young girls and boys in western style* at the beat of the drum and other instrumental music. It goes on at any place and at any time in the market place or in a narrow street stopping the easy flow of traffic. It is in vogue for almost twenty-five years and most people feel that they enjoy that kind of activity. Dance and music are aesthetic activities. They are certainly of great utility at certain occasions and may bring benefits when performed at a particular time and place. But I have apprehensions about this kind of activity performed by our young men and women. As the beat of the drum accelerates during a marriage procession, the heat of emotions also increases in the hearts of the young people. How aesthetic it looks when the young boys and girls at the tune of some indecent movie-song dance furiously to captivate the attention of the public! One can imagine such scenes and reckon how good their aesthetic value could be. I am not totally condemning boys and girls dancing at the occasion of a marriage. I simply mean that these activities must be performed in a most aesthetic sense at certain places only (surely not the marketplace), preferably at the bride's place. Besides, as far as possible such dances must accompany decent music and songs but certainly not the type of songs like *'choli kay peechai kya hai'* (what is there behind the blouse of a woman?)

Besides the customs that have lately been accepted by the people, some of the beliefs that were strongly held dearer and true by the people in the past are getting weaker day by day. One of the distinctive features of Hinduism has been the belief in *samsara*. The rounds of birth, death and rebirth are understood as a cycle of transmigration from one living form into another. This belief is first mentioned in the *Brihadaranyaka*

Upanishad. It says that after death a human being may be reborn in a higher or lower form of life. The belief in transmigration is also strongly connected with the belief in *karma*. It denotes both an action and its good and bad effects. The *karma* built up through the acts done in a previous life is a determining factor towards the condition of the present life, which in turn affects the rebirth in the next life. All this serene ideology is not getting much attention of the people these days. As a result, the values connected with the idea of birth and rebirth have lost individual's attention. The present circumstances are quite dismal in that respect. As a result, there has been a great change in a Hindu's way of thinking and his day-to-day conduct. Whether there is any hell or not, but the fear that wrong conduct would throw people in the fire of hell certainly used to stop them acting in an immoral manner.

Perhaps, it is the impact of the Western education or sudden changes in the way of life of the people. They feel 'the present' to be more important and real today than the future. Consequently, they don't approve of the idea to live for future. As a result, the values that made them commit actions, which would secure their future well, are becoming less important for them. Formerly, people due to fear of losing a place in the heaven would always remember to act benevolently. They would think many times before acting immorally. In fact, the *Gita* laid a lot of stress on man's duty and emphasized to act without the desire of any results or gain from their actions. This kind of idea is gradually getting faded. '*Why should I work if I don't get benefit from my actions?* This thought has become more important and dearer these days. Thus, the belief that there is another life after death has been losing grounds. With that, many new ideas have been introduced in one's daily life. One likes to work now only for the sake of benefits and gains rather than anything else.

So far we have not discussed the *Carvaka* school of thought, which influenced a Hindu mind quite casually. People in the past hardly accepted such an ideology. It seems that the Carvaka's view *'eat, drink and be merry'* is gradually getting popular these days. People like to enjoy their lives and don't believe much in the welfare of others. Most people like to fulfil their own interests than the interests and happiness of others. Consequently, the *institution of family, which included the parents also, has become vulnerable.* Young man of today likes to live with his children and wife only than to live with his parents. It is resulting in less security and goodwill in the family unit. When older people used to live with their grandchildren, most of them cared for them (grandchildren) and desired them to imbibe values. Not only they desired the children to learn good habits and values, they acted accordingly too. Thus, they automatically created a value-oriented environment, which cannot be cultivated by lectures and talks. This kind of transformation in the way of a Hindu family has brought tremendous changes in a Hindu's way of living. While pulling the burden of the family and fulfilling the daily needs of all the members, the young head of the family feels frustrated at times. He is unable to find the right way in want of any kind of guidance from his/her elders as the new definition of the family is devoid of the old man and the woman. The idea of a nuclear family without parents has thus weakened the value system of a family to a certain extent. These are some of the recent developments that the modern Hindu society is experiencing these days. There are other ill-practices too, besides what have been indicated here above. Some of them were observed while visiting the holy places and working with the Hindu individuals. They are unfolded here under.

Apathy towards Visiting Temples

It has been a recent phenomenon that quite a number of educated Hindu individuals have developed apathy towards the Hindu temples. Consequently, neither they visit any temples nor they much approve of others' visiting there. They cough at the people who express any desire to go to a temple. Perhaps because of that or due to any other reasons, the percentage of the young people visiting temples has reduced tremendously in the modern age. Not only the non-visitors reckon it a waste of their valuable time to visiting a temple, they also don't believe in any kind of worshipping. Why one should go to a temple when he/she possesses less or no belief in worshipping? Some don't visit a temple because they hold that home is a better place to keep in touch with God. No doubt, if we can cultivate worshipping and meditating at home for some time each day, it would be an excellent act towards practising religion. But those who say that they hardly get time to meditate or to practise any kind of worship at home, they are either simply lethargic or apathetic to that kind of practice. Some may feel bad by neglecting these duties in every day life, but they don't act that way due to lethargy or adequate will. Yet there are really people who try to act that way and find time to visit a temple once in a week. But the time they give to God is hardly a couple of minutes.

Once while I was sitting with one of my student-friends at a temple-stairs, I observed a car slowly stopping near the temple. A gentleman alighted from it and gradually advanced towards the temple. As soon as he was able to have a glimpse of the statue, he saluted it for a couple of seconds and departed at once. I don't denounce any one's way(s) of worshipping but could one really pay his/her respects to God by saluting Him for a few seconds only? I reckon we need a little more time to make prayer and offerings. Praying is the most sacred activity of an individual through which he/she is able to establish a close communion with Him. It needs more time than the particular individual was able to provide.

In fact, when we are praying, we are not giving any thing to God but simply seeking something for us. It is true that one may not need to visit any temple to offer prayers. He/she may do it at home quite regularly. But a temple is a place, which automatically creates an environment of love for God. I have seen people prostrating while proceeding to reach the doors of a temple. That kind of activity could be a kind of showing off before others, but after reaching the temple and prostrating in front of the statue in perfect faith and intimate devotion, could not be an act of show if the individual starts concentrating on the greatness of God. It used to be a regular practice of most of the Hindu individuals to visit temples of their choice in the past. Students would do it most regularly during examination days. They would do it more regularly when they grow adults as they see their elders practising worshipping regularly. Unfortunately, it is a recent trend to hold oneself from visiting the holy places and avoiding going to the temples. Apathy to visiting the temples may gradually take us away from the spirit of the religion. Some may say it is not, but I strongly feel it is.

Corruption at the Holy Places

One of the causes of people's apathy in visiting the temples and the holy places is the corrupt practices that are rampant there. I have already discussed some of the corrupt ways and practices that you may experience at the sacred places. But there are other unholy practices raging in the temples. Most of these unwanted methods and ways have mainly one motive behind. It is extracting money from the pilgrims and the temple-visitors in different ways. What about selling the *prasadam* (the remains of God's offerings) on phenomenal rates to the pilgrims? At times the visitors and the pilgrims, who visit a holy place or a temple of great repute with profound devotion, are harassed in different ways at the temple complex. Not only they are forced to purchase the *prasadam* at the phenomenal rates, they are also compelled to do various other activities supposed to be religious in order to cleanse their sins. It generates a kind of dislike and apathy in the minds of the visitors who often visit such places with utmost devotion and emotional enthusiasm.

Yet there is another corrupt practice which is a sin in itself. Neither the government authorities nor the temple management pay any attention towards it. When a great number of pilgrims visit a holy place at particular occasions, total chaos is seen all over the place. No attention is paid towards hygienic conditions of the temple. Consequently, unclean conditions that include filth, dust and every kind of repulsive sight, become the host of the visitors' eyes. It is said that cleanliness is next to godliness. But it is almost missing within and outside the temple or a holy place.

I reckon it is the management of the place, which is totally responsible to keep the place clean. A great number of beggars often infest these places making the visitors' movement difficult around the temple. Lepers are no exception to it. Can the temple management take care of those poor beggars and the lepers? Is there someone who would care for the devoted visitors without much ado and provide them a welcoming and holy sight within the temple complex so that they like to visit there again?

Lack of Availability of the Experts

It is really so unfortunate that there is a great want of the experts who would earnestly fulfil the requirements to perform rituals methodically at each opportunity. For example, the auspicious occasions like naming ceremony of a child, performance of a marriage, or accomplishing the last rites of one's parents or when one enters one's newly constructed house etc., experts are required to perform the ceremony. For each such occasion, a written text is available. Most of this text is supposed to be inherited from the past. A true pundit (*purohit*) always carries the right kind of scriptures to perform the ceremony. But lately, it has been observed that most of these ceremonies go either partly fulfilled or unfulfilled in the real sense, as there are a very few experts to get the work done correctly. What is mostly performed is the replica of the ritual and most of the so-called experts (*purohits*) who carry the text with them in an indigenous manner hardly know how to fulfil the rituals with the help of the right texts. I remember a marriage-scene when the bridegroom was waiting to sit under the *mandap* (a kind of temporary hut) with the bride to perform the marriage rituals. When the *purohits* were ready to accomplish the ceremony and to fulfil the rituals, they started chanting Sanskrit *slokas* (verses). But one of the *purohits*, a qualified Sanskrit scholar, started reciting *slokas* slowly. It is often observed that during a marriage ceremony the *purohits* chant the *slokas* very loudly so that all who are attending the ceremony may be a witness to the occasion and along with the *purohits'* chanting of the Sanskrit verses they also bless the occasion. The said Sanskrit scholar, who was also a Sanskrit teacher in a government school, was reciting the verses meekly because he was not well versed with the procedure. He did not possess the right kind of textbook too. Therefore, with a low confidence he recited the verses in a slow voice. He knew it well that he was simply chanting the *Gayatri mantra* repeatedly. Thus, to hide his inadequacy he mixed his voice with the other *purohits*. It so happened that one of his students accompanying the marriage party could decipher the meaning of the low tone of the Sanskrit scholar. For a few minutes he observed the *purohit*, but after that he could not resist asking him whether the *purohit* was reciting from the right text. It suddenly created a great uproar as the Sanskrit scholar who was officially one of the *purohits* (most of the time at such occasions there are two purohits to perform the ritual.) to perform the marriage ritual, could not tolerate the remark of his own student. To cut the story short, it became evident that the said *purohit* was not reciting the right kind of verses meant for the occasion.

If the reader remembers some of the details contained in the first chapter of this book, they would recall how the Brahmins were jealously committed to practise each verse contained in the *Vedas*. It was one of their commitments and there lay their expertise. That was the reason that during the Vedic-Brahmanic period the Brahmins or the *purohits* conspicuously dominated the society for a long time. It is so unfortunate that there are very few schools where training in ritualistic performances and methodology is given in our country. There are a few good schools at Benaras (Uttar Pradesh) which offer such training to the desired scholars but gradually the number of such schools has reduced in want of good scholars. Most recently during the beginning of the new millennium the Minister of Education and Human Resources made a move to introduce certain new dimensions in education. He tried to make provision of such kind of education which would provide proper education to the desired scholars to become experts in the ritualistic methodology, astrology and the related fields. It initiated quite a large opposition in the Indian Parliament and a great uproar against this kind of move was witnessed against the Minister's designs and intentions.

Some parliamentarians have condemned this kind of development naming it *'Bhagvakaran of Education'*. How much such a move of the Members of the Parliament is right, cannot be assessed right now. Only the future can tell about it. If the efforts of the Minister of Education are well intentioned, they are surely going to bring good results in future in the sense that the dearth of the experts who could perform the rituals methodically would come to an end. It is certainly improper to introduce politics in the field of education for it would bring colossal devastation, which can hardly ever be repaired. But if someone's move to introduce certain essential courses to end the dearth in a coveted field, is well intentioned, it should be welcomed. Perhaps, it is on account of lack of experts in the ritualistic methodology that quite a large number of educated masses have developed apathy towards such activities and the *purohits* as well. They know it well that there are hardly a few *purohits* who know their job very earnestly. Such *purohits* try to fulfil the auspicious occasions with any short ritualistic activity whether it befits the occasion or not. Consequently, a great number of educated people complain that they have lack of time and, therefore, they don't wish to indulge with long traditional rituals.

Whatever be the case, it is certain that there is a great need of experts who could accomplish the rituals in the most earnest way. If there were more true scholars, it would restore confidence of the masses and help certain practices in Hinduism go smoothly. I reckon constant research in this direction must be introduced to perpetuate the cause of Hinduism. There is still time to arrest the failing interests and falling standards. We all need to put adequate efforts to make Hinduism the only best religion of the world. For that we need to focus on its inadequacies and to bring back all its best dimensions that have been lost so far. It would certainly require introducing the best that could reinstall it on a much higher seat.

Whether Truly Liberal!

One of the important matters related with the real growth of

Hinduism is the issue, 'whether a Hindu is truly liberal.' It is such a question that most of the followers of the religion may not like to reply negatively, but a Hindu though liberal, is highly conservative in many ways. It is true that a Hindu could visit a church and attend the service on Sundays with his friends. He may even go to a mosque if permitted because he does not fear to get converted or polluted on account of such visits. So far he is very liberal. He is not dogmatic as far as many Hindu practices are concerned. He may often find a short cut to accomplish a ritual or perform a ceremony. But he is very conservative within his own fold. Most astonishingly, he is conservative when it is the occasion of the marriage of his son or daughter. Most Hindus are almost fanatically traditional if they are asked to give away their daughter to a family, which doesn't belong to their caste. So is the case at the time of one's son's marriage. A Hindu would always prefer to marry his son in a Hindu family of the same caste and of higher status.

A Hindu is also conservative in other matters too. Many Hindu families would not like to dine with the people of other community, especially belonging to other religion or of low caste. Although there has been a slight decline in this narrow traditional outlook, many a times a lot of embarrassment is experienced when a Hindu declines to eat with a person of low caste or poor status. Is it not very strange that a Hindu, who is very liberal in so many matters, is highly conventional at so many occasions and creates problems of immense nature? As a result, the Hindus, who belong to a lower caste, often feel hurt and humiliated. It was the reason that the Constitution of India made a strong provision for the protection and betterment of the downtrodden. The caste system, though initially created in line with one's vocation, has done more damage to the entire Hindu community in the recent times. I have witnessed painfully many times how some *dalits* (low caste Hindus) on account of humiliation and insults have relinquished their religion and converted into other religions. I quote from Bhaichand Patel's article, published in the *Hindustan Times* a couple of years back. The article titled, "Goodbye Hinduism, hello Buddhism" clearly conveys how frustrated low caste

Hindus opt to convert to other religions. Bhaichand Patel remarks, "The caste system is peculiar to Hinduism in the sense that nothing remotely like it is found in any other religion. One can understand the anger and frustration the *dalits* feel about their position in society. The religion leaves little space for social fusion." Mr. Patel wrote this article when someone, named Ram Raj, a dalit leader, relinquished Hindu religion and converted to Buddhism. I am really anguished to report the morning news on the Aaj Tak channel on television that 250 Hindus converted to Christianity in Tamil Nadu. All such kind of rapid conversions from Hinduism to Christianity and Buddhism is being caused primarily on account of the conduct and constant hatred of the upper caste Hindus against the lower caste Hindus. Keeping all such matters in view can we really consider a Hindu liberal in the true sense?

What Minimum a Hindu is Required to Do?

I reckon each Hindu has some kind of duty towards the religion. What that duty should be, can be better understood through a formal and comprehensive research. But whatever I have been able to discover in this direction in a year's span through informal interviews of the Hindu community in India and abroad, is given here below for the reader's reference. In fact, my main focus was to learn the views of the Hindus across the country and from abroad for a long time. I only asked them what minimum practice(s) they would like every Hindu to perform each day or each week so that Hinduism may not only survive but also progress perpetually in the future. It seemed to them a difficult question to reply. A Hindu even if he/she does not visit a temple or does not meditate or read from the *Ramayana*, remains a Hindu by the virtue of being born in a Hindu family. So, he does not care for what is required of him. Therefore, the question which I asked, though simple, seemed to most of them difficult. But after scratching their heads for a couple of minutes they said a few things, which seemed to be relevant. Their common views are listed here under.

Most of the people who were interviewed confided that each Hindu must practise the following every day:

1. Meditate for at least fifteen minutes each day any time of the day suitable to the individual.
2. Participate in the festivals like Holi and Depawali whole-heartedly.
3. Must read regularly from the *Bhagvad Gita* or the *Ramayana* each day for a few minutes. Some suggested that text, containing the best from most of the holy books, should be prepared and all should read it regularly.
4. One must participate in the religious *sammelans* (gatherings) whenever an opportunity is available.
5. Each Hindu family must keep a *tulsi* plant in the house and if possible it may be worshipped as women used to do so in the past.
6. *Ramleela* should be played in each town and hamlet during *Dashehra* as it was done in the past. People must visit such plays. It will not only provide entertainment but will also help in the development of values among them.
7. Aradhana (worshipping and concentration) of one's personal God for some time each day any time is imperative.
8. Worshipping five great powers such as the sun, Ganesha, Kali (Shakti), Krishna and Rama each day whenever one gets time.
9. Practice *Yoga* every day for at least fifteen minutes earnestly.
10. Instead of greeting people with 'Hai', as is customary in the West, a Hindu must greet each other with 'Namastay' or 'Jai Ramji ki/Jai Sri Ram or Jai Sri Krishna.'

There can be more suggestions in this respect that may create some kind of insight and affinity towards the religion. I reckon most important is the participation of individuals in the activities that are connected with the religion. Most people, who were interviewed by me, reflected that every Hindu must meditate for ten to fifteen minutes each day, preferably in the morning. That meditation may be to empty one's mind with any kind of thoughts, or to concentrate on OM, which has a very comprehensive meaning. One may concentrate on one's personal God too at that time. This kind of exercise will keep one connected with the religion, which is absolutely imperative.

Redefining Hinduism

At the concluding stage, I would like to define again what are the basics of this august religion. In spite of constant hurdles, oppositions and impediments, it has been going on timelessly. Although there has been a slight departure in its practices, the basic beliefs with slight changes stay for good. Thus, the religion has been perpetuating for many thousand years.

In spite of the fact that it may lack few things like any other great religion, it possesses something unusual, grand and unparalleled that cannot be matched with the greatest religions of the world. Imagine the period when the *Vedas* were created. The *Vedas* existed a few thousand years before the creation of most of the other holy books or religion. They say the *Vedas* were revealed. Even if it is not true (those who don't accept it they cannot disprove it too), who can deny the amount of truth and knowledge contained in the *Vedas*. Just think dispassionately how the Hindu mind discovered such astonishing facts about the universe, self and the Creator. Let us keep aside for a minute the belief in the existence of Brahman, as many atheistic minds would not accept that kind of idea. But can anyone deny the facts discovered about one's soul, life and *samsara*? Perhaps no one can. When Buddha discovered the Four Cardinal Truths, it was absolutely a true observation about the *samsara* and life. None had its inkling prior to Buddha although the facts already existed. Likewise, in the second chapter of *Srimad Bhagvad Gita*, Sri Krishna describing the self, unfolds:

> **This Self cannot be cut, nor burnt, nor wetted, nor dried.**
> **Changeless, all-pervading, unmoving, immovable, the self is eternal. (2.24)***

If one wants to know more about the Self and its characteristics, one needs to read from the great Jain Munis' whose description about it is great. The Jains define *Jiva* or *atman* as a conscious substance. "*Atman* in this world is known as *Jiva*. It has vital and physical, mental and sensuous powers. In its pure condition, *Jiva* has pure knowledge and vision i.e., Nirvikalpa and Savikalpa *Jnana* (knowledge)." Thus, the portrayal of *Jiva* by the Jains is more pointed and descriptive. Defining its characteristics, the Jains consider that the "Jiva is self-illuminated and illuminates other things also. It is eternal and it pervades the whole body." (R.N.S.).

Such a description of the soul is the strength of Indian philosophy and the religion. It is really so difficult to define or to conceive the soul so distinctly as the Jains conceived it much ahead of the spread of many other religions. In fact, Jainism as a philosophy is quite distinctive and has its own identity but it can only be seen as an offshoot of Hinduism. Basically it is much influenced by the Vedic traditions and thought. Such a description of *atman* is quite akin to the description of the soul contained in the *Gita*, which says:

> **This (soul) is unborn, eternal, changeless, ever-Itself. (2.20)***

Whatever may be the case, defining the self (soul) is quite an uphill task, which cannot be accomplished by ordinary minds. Hinduism has that privilege as well as depth and, therefore, the idea of soul has a strong foothold. It would not be possible for any person, religion or anti-social activist to eradicate the idea of the existence of a soul from the minds of the people who belong to Hinduism. Such a view about it is still rampant among the Hindu masses and, therefore, in line with the Vedantic tradition they go on trying to seek ways to purify it and to seek Brahman.

Besides conceiving the soul so distinctly, Hinduism has the privilege to see the facts about life very precisely. The Gita says, '*Of that which is born, death is certain; of that which is dead, birth is certain.*' Thus, the belief in transmigration, which is deeply implanted in a Hindu mind, has absolutely influenced one's way of life and moral perspective. As a consequence, the religion has suggested a clear way to act in one's life so that one may gradually be free from the fetters of death and re-birth. Suggesting how to attain the eternal bliss in life and to cut off the chains of death and re-birth, the *Gita* suggests the way of action, which can certainly transcend one to the realm of eternal happiness. It says, *Thy right is to work only: but never to the fruits there of.* It is such a *mantra* that if comprehended properly, it can surely transport one to a much higher plane. Some of these notions are not merely beliefs but are the basic facts about life and *samsara*. If you comprehend these notions distinctly, you may attain the most coveted peace of mind unquestioningly, and thereby attain unending happiness. It is also the stage of total liberation. There lies the strength of the religion. There lies the greatness of Hinduism.

Most people who have faith in the religion do believe in the *Gita's* precepts relating to the soul and the *samsara* as well as in the concept of 'duty for duty's sake.' Much more than all that there is something more that Hinduism can claim to be one of the best religions of the world. It suggests three-fold ways to attain liberation or *moksha*. These are the *path of knowledge*, the *path of action* and the *path of bhakti*. We have already discussed these ways in details in the third chapter of this book. But I would like to reflect a little more on *Yoga*, which is also considered a way to liberation. The importance of *Yoga* as a technique of purifying the mind is accepted even in the *Vedanta*. On account of its lucid techniques and positive results, it is also becoming very popular in the Western world, besides the Asian sub-continent.

Yoga philosophy specializes in the presentation of means to achieve liberation. Ever since the time of the *Upanishads* right up to the present day, most Indian philosophers from Yajnavalkya to Sri Aurovindo, have taken into account *Yoga* to be the most potent and indispensable method to attain liberation. In fact, *Yoga* is the practical way for the realization of the theoretical ideas contained in the *Samkhya* philosophy. Both *Samkhya* and *Yoga* philosophies hold that liberation can be attained only by knowledge. Attainment of this knowledge requires gradual control over body, mind, senses, intellect and ego so that the pure self may be realized. But the realization of the pure self requires the awareness that the self is beyond the body, mind, senses, intellect and ego etc. It is beyond space and time, liberated and eternal too.

I don't desire to drag the reader into the details of various techniques of *Yoga*. Yogic exercises are contained in several books on *Yoga* wherein with the help of figures and sketches various Yogic postures have been projected brilliantly, including their advantages. I would like to mention at this juncture that it is certainly one of the best ways to attain peace of mind and strength of body. There lies the greatness of Hinduism. I don't think there is any philosophy or religion in the world that has enumerated such techniques for obtaining peace of mind, happiness and liberation as *Yoga* has unfolded. In view of that, Hinduism is gorgeous and excellent. I, therefore, wish to appeal to all the Hindu minded people whether living abroad or within the country that they should feel happy to be a Hindu and practise each day at least any one of the activities mentioned under the sub-head *What Minimum a Hindu is Required to Do?* It would make him/her feel united with the religion, and enhance the age-old culture that has been flourishing for such a long time, in spite of various jolts during the last thousand years.

People have always accused Hinduism that it does not believe in one God. There are thousands of gods and goddesses that the Hindus worship, while most people of the world believe in one God only. I reckon those who accuse Hinduism on that account, they are misinformed. They have never tried to comprehend the religion properly. For behind that sort of plurality, there lies a belief that the ultimate God is one, Brahman, Who manifests in various forms to benefit the people and to bring comfort and happiness to them when they need it actually. Can one really assess the greatness of this age-old religion, which though appears to be practising plurality, has always held the belief in the sovereignty of Brahman only?

Before concluding this small work, I wish to remind each Hindu individual that he must never feel low in being a Hindu. For one who is a Hindu in the real sense is one of the best specimen of a human being, as he surely believes in caring more for others and possesses unending faith in *dharma*. He does not only believe in the existence of Brahman, the Creator of this universe, but also holds absolutely that whenever there will be chaos in moral terms, God will incarnate on this earth and ratify the ills by His will and actions. Sri Krishna narrates in the *Gita*:

> **Whenever, O descendant of Bharat, there is decline of Dharma,**
> **and rise of Adharma, then I body Myself forth. (4.7)***

It is perhaps on account of the belief that Brahman is the Ultimate Truth and He intervenes with human affairs whenever required, most Hindu minded people willfully go on indulging with the *bhakti marg* (the way of devotion). They believe that it is the only and an immediate way to attain Brahman and happiness as well. Examples of that kind are plentiful not only in the Indian sub-continent but in abroad also where people of different religions found the *bhakti* procedure as the surest way to reach God's realm. It is perhaps on account of that insistent belief among the people that a great number of Hindu families do possess a small temple in their houses where they regularly pray whenever they get time or at a prescribed time.

It is agonizing that the caste divisions are great impediments in the smooth flow and propagation of the religion, but most people who are liberal in their outlook and conduct, especially the educated and enlightened people, don't let the caste system get hold of their minds. As a result, inter-caste marriages among different castes in Hindus are becoming quite popular. This could be a little departure from the old traditions but it is a healthy sign to make the religion thrive and perpetuate against the odds of conservatism which at a point of time in the Hindu history was popular and potent.

The belief in the immortality of the soul and to shun the chain of death and rebirth has never departed from the Hindu mind. Perhaps, it will never depart as most of those who have faith in this religion desire to get salvation (*moksha*) and wish to get redeemed from the fetters of birth and rebirth. Consequently, in the subconscious mind of each Hindu the precept of *karma* resides. As the belief in the sovereignty of Brahman is deep rooted in a Hindu believer, he always transcends from the so-called narrow 'belief in many gods and goddesses' for he knows that the Ultimate Truth is Brahman only.

Books Consulted

1. Anthony S. Merecatante (1988): *The Facts on File Encyclopaedia of World Mythology And Legend*, New York, Facts on file.
2. A.P. Sharma (2001): *Concept of Freedom*, San Jose, Authors Choice Press.
3. Fritiof Capra (1976): *The Tao of Physics*, New York, Batam Books.
4. Gavin Flod (1996): *An Introduction to Hinduism*, Cambridge, Camridge University Press.
5. Jawaharlal Nehru (1946): *The Discovery of India*, New York, The John Day Company.
6. John R. Hinnels (1984): *The Facts on File Dictionary of Religious* (Ed.), New York, Facts on File.
7. Keith Crim (Gen.Ed.) (1981): *A Bingdon Dictionary of Living Religious*, Nashville, Abingdon.
8. Norman Anderson (1975): *The World's Religious*, Michigan, William B. Eerdmans Publishing Company.
9. Peter Bishop and Michael Darton (1987): *The Encyclopaedia of World Faiths*, New York, Facts of File Publication.
10. Peter D'Epiro & Mary Desmond Pinkowish (1998): *What are the Seven Wonders of the World*, New York, Doubleday.
11. R.S. Sharma (1972): *Indian Philosophy*, New Delhi, Longman Ltd.
12. S.G.E. Brandon (1970): *Dictionary of Comparative Religions*, New York, Charles Scribner's Sons.
13. *Sri Ramacaritamanasa* (1995): Gita Press Gorakhpur, India.
14. *Srimadbhagawat-Sudha-Sagar* (1995): Gita Press Gorakhpur, India.
15. Stephen Mitchell (1988): *Bhagvad Gita*, New York, Harmony Books.
16. Swami Swarupananda (1969): *Srimad Bhagwad Gita*, Calcutta, Advaita Ashram.
17. Virinica Ions (1984): *Indian Mythology*, New York, Peter Bedrick Books.

Index